Splend
of the
Gala

Ken and Jean Smith

ERGO PRESS
Publishing for Northumberland

SPLENDOUR OF THE GALA

First Published by Ergo Press
5 St Mary's Chare
Hexham
Northumberland
NE46 1NQ

ergo.press@yahoo.co.uk
www.ergopress.com

ISBN: 978-0-9557510-7-3

Cover graphics by Slim Palmer
www.slimpalmer.com

Printed by Elanders Hindson Ltd
New York Business Park
Newcastle upon Tyne
NE27 0YT

Written, published and printed in the North East of England

TABLE OF CONTENTS

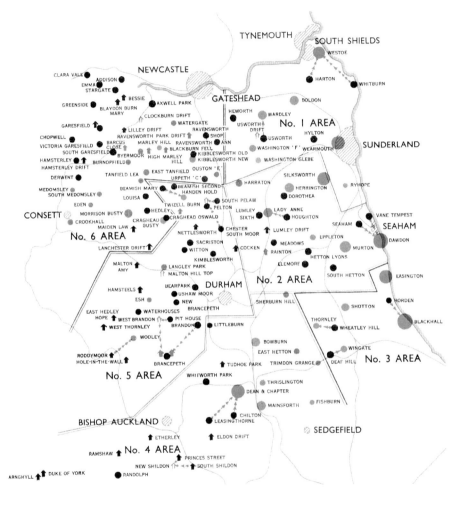

FOREWORD

In this book, the authors tackle the phenomenon of the Durham Miners' Gala which, remarkably, has gone from strength to strength since the closure of the last deep-mined Durham colliery, Wearmouth, in 1993. They chronicle the early days of the Durham Miners' Association and the formation of the early days of struggle, through the hard times of the 1920s right through to the present day – a truly remarkable journey.

They capture the pride and dignity of the mining communities, their joy at being involved in the largest working-class demonstration in the UK and the great colour and sound of the colliery bands accompanying their standards into the city of Durham.

It is some one hundred and forty years since the first Miners' Gala in Wharton Park and it would take many volumes to cover the entire history and splendour of this great event, but the book relates the annual story, from the selection of banner carriers, the early morning parade through the villages, the journey to Durham and the return home after a very long but satisfactory day.

Bands and banners are potent icons of mining communities and nowhere more so than in the Durham mining communities. Even today we are witnessing a resurgence of local groups raising funds to have new banners made, or old ones lovingly restored, to take pride of place in their communities and to remind the younger generation of how important coal was in the lives of their villages and their people.

Many schools become involved in the design of banners and undertake projects on mining. It is to be hoped that this will encourage the youngsters to attend and support a heritage and history built on struggle, a struggle that enabled the miners to build communities that believed in people helping one another, working together and assisting people in their time of need. Their values led to the Big Meeting – long may it continue.

Dave Hopper,
General Secretary,
Durham Miners' Association

LAND OF THE PITMEN
THE GALA BEGINS

Britain's most famed gathering of pitmen, the Durham Miners' Gala, has survived the closure of every deep mine in the North-East. It is an event which has reflected, over its many years of existence, the essentially humanitarian values of the miners and the friendly spirit of their communities.

The Gala began in Victorian times as a demonstration of the miners' solidarity and was intended to send a clear message to the employers that the men were united and determined to obtain their 'reets'. They were seeking fair treatment, improved pay, safer working conditions, compensation for injury and support for widows and families in the event of a man's death as the result of his pit work. It was essentially a trade union gathering.

However, the Gala also developed into a major family day out, an occasion for fun and enjoyment, and an opportunity for people throughout the many pit communities of County Durham to meet and socialise. Since the closure of all the region's pits, the Gala has also evolved into a celebration of the North East's mining heritage.

That heritage is as deep and rich as the seams that evoked it; coal mining has touched the lives of a huge number of people throughout County Durham. Indeed, the area might be called "Land of the Pitmen" rather than "Land of the Prince Bishops". Coal was the lifeblood of thousands between the North Pennines and the North Sea and today many people still living within the old boundaries of the county are descended from miners.

But although it was the economic mainstay of the Durham economy, coal was also the source of heartache, of struggles, ordeals and great loss of life. However, through these many traumas, the people of the pit communities displayed a cheerful resilience, warmth and strength of character, underpinned by the strong influences of Christianity, socialist ideals and trade unionism.

This warmth and these principles shine through on the colourful union lodge banners held high at the Durham Miners' Gala. Painted on both sides, they express values which transcend narrow materialism; they tell the story of a people's determination to overcome injustice and to care for each other in the face of hardship and tragedy.

The first Gala was held at Wharton Park, Durham, on August 12, 1871, although every Gala since then has been held at Durham's old racecourse by the River Wear. Around 4,000 to 5,000 pitmen and their families attended, and the event has taken place every year since this inception, apart from 1915-1918 and 1940-45 (during the two world wars), the lockout of 1921, the depressed year of 1922, the Great Lockout of 1926 and in 1984 during the Great Strike against pit closures.

Attendances have varied, but the Gala always attracts many thousands. A record estimated attendance of around 300,000 was reported in July 1951, when the Labour Prime Minister Clement Attlee was the main guest speaker. During other years in the 1950s it was estimated around 200,000-250,000 attended; the narrow streets of the city centre overflowing with supporters.

At the first 'Big Meeting' or 'Durham Big Meeting', as this extraordinary event came to be known, the platform was decorated with the banner of Thornley Lodge of the Durham Miners' Association, the pitmen's union, founded in 1869. Thornley was an early stronghold of mining trade unionism: in late 1843, men at this colliery went on strike against excessive pay deductions and fines. The men were accused of breaking their Bond, a hated annual contract which forced them by law to work for their employer for a year without any guarantee of work. They were cleared on a technicality after a brilliant defence by W.P. Roberts, known as the 'Pitman's Attorney General' or 'Pitman's Attorney'.

At that first Gala, another banner in the arena bore the message, 'A fair day's wage for a fair day's work'. However, the lighter side of the gala was also evident – a contest was held for the bands, and various athletic sports took place. Some residents of Durham had feared that the miners would cause trouble in the city, but their fears proved groundless and the day was entirely peaceful.

The second Gala, in 1872, saw the racecourse used as the venue for the first time. Miners were present from 180 collieries – an amazing total –

and at this date membership of the Durham Miners' Association (DMA) numbered around 35,000.

The Big Meeting was addressed by Alexander McDonald, then president of the National Association of Miners, and by the Durham miners' pioneering leader William Crawford, who is sometimes credited with conceiving the idea of the Gala. If he did so, he is likely to have been inspired by the major North East pit strikes of 1831, 1832 and 1844 when mass meetings with banners demonstrated the men's unity.

It is of interest that one of the first references to the use of banners by the miners is contained in an account of the 1831 dispute, written by Richard Fynes in his book *The Miners of Northumberland and Durham*, published 1873:

On the 21st April (1831), a large meeting of miners was held at Jarrow, each colliery bearing a banner, with the name of the colliery and various mottoes.

On the 13th August, in the same year, the miners of the two counties of Northumberland and Durham, met on Boldon Fell... During the forenoon the roads in the vicinity of the meeting place presented an unusual bustle, the men walking in procession from the different collieries, bearing flags and banners and accompanied by bands of music. The banners were numerous, and of the gayest description, nearly all being embellished with a painted design, and with a motto more or less connected with the recent struggle between the miners and their employers.

A resolution passed by those present at the second Gala stressed the importance of arbitration – a clear reference to the success of the union's talks with the employers earlier that year when the oppressive yearly Bond had been abolished and a 20% wage rise achieved.

In 1897, the pitmen and their families took part in a service at Durham Cathedral on the afternoon of Gala day, so instituting the annual *Miners' Festival Service*, which became a lasting feature of the Big Meeting; the 100th service was held in July 2009.

Miners and Bishops

The development of the friendly relationship between the miners and the Anglican Church at Durham is perhaps a little surprising, since many pitmen and their families were Methodists, whether Primitive, Wesleyan or Independent. Regardless of this difference, over a period of more than a century since that first service of 1897 several Bishops of Durham have expressed strong sympathies with the miners and their communities in their struggle for better conditions, for improved safety and for the preservation of their jobs and communities.

The relationship with the cathedral clerics began in 1892 when the Bishop of Durham, Brooke Foss Westcott, *left,* interceded between the pitmen and employers during a major strike against a wage reduction. He invited both sides to the Bishop's residence, Auckland Palace, where he urged a settlement of their differences. The two parties first held a joint meeting, and then split up to consider their positions in separate rooms. According to John Wilson (*A History of the Durham Miners' Association 1870-1904*), "the Bishop passed from room to room full of solicitude for a settlement". Although the strike failed to achieve its original objective, the amiable cleric did succeed in persuading the owners to drop their demand for a 13.5% reduction in wages. Instead, the cut was lowered to 10%, the percentage which the owners had originally demanded; it was during the strike that they had raised their demand to 13.5%.

For his efforts to achieve a settlement of the strike, Brooke Foss Westcott was dubbed the 'Miners' Bishop'. Westcott also played an important role in the establishment of the *Durham Aged Mineworkers' Homes Association*, which was founded in the 1890s and today still provides homes for ex-pitmen and their wives or widows, as well as others, throughout the county and in parts of Tyne and Wear. We will hear more about the miners' bishops later in this book.

George Robson and the Gala

George Robson, retired financial secretary of Durham Area of the National Union of Mineworkers (NUM), has been the main organiser of the Durham Miners' Gala for more than thirty years, having first become involved with making the arrangements at the age of twenty seven. George, the son of a Boldon Colliery pitman, is an accomplished artist and a significant number of his works are on the Gala theme. He was first taken to the Big Meeting as a boy, when he marched with his father, a strong trade unionist, behind the lodge banner along streets packed with a sea of people.

This great event is an outpouring of the miners' spirit. It is famed throughout Britain and is now almost legendary. "The Gala goes from strength to strength despite the closure of the mines," George declares. The spirit of the pitmen and their communities has outlived the destruction of the industry wrought in the 1980s and 1990s.

George points out that the Big Meeting, which for most of its history has been held in July (generally on the second Saturday of the month), is the largest and most colourful miners' event in the world. It attracts visitors from other parts of the globe, including musicians. The list includes delegations of miners from Russia, Australia, South Africa and Belgium. Bands from America and Australia have played in the parade. Representatives from Bulgaria, Hungary and Cuba have also been among the international visitors.

Most other such events have faded away with the demise of the pits, but Durham's annual display of pride and togetherness continues unabated. The former mining villages and towns have rediscovered their heritage. George explains: "With the closures, people in the villages began looking inward and asked themselves the question, 'Why are we here?' The answer was: 'Because of the pit.' They decided to celebrate this fact."

One of the most impressive developments from this realisation has been the formation of community groups to replicate or restore old union lodge banners and parade them at the Gala and other events, as symbols of pride in what the miners did for Britain and the world while carrying out one of the most dangerous jobs imaginable. They are also symbols of the miners' close comradeship and of the strong community spirit that persists in villages and towns throughout the Durham coalfield. Indeed, the banners are emblems of each community as well as being icons of mining trade unionism. A considerable number of old banners are stored at Red Hill, the Durham miners' union headquarters, and others are kept by the lodges, many of which are still in existence as they help to continue the work of winning compensation for ex-miners affected by industrial diseases and injury.

George stresses the miners' record of concern for others. Contributions paid from their wages went into union welfare funds, both local and area-wide, for the benefit of deserving causes, including hospitals and the homes for aged miners. The good causes chosen to receive local funds were selected by the lodges and voted on by the membership. He points out that around 95% of the funding for the Big Meeting comes from the DMA; the remainder is donated by *Unison* and the *North East and Cumbria Co-op*, together with a number of smaller contributions.

The Miners' Festival Service

To this day, every year, the Bishop of Durham dedicates and blesses new union lodge banners at the Miners' Festival Service. The new standards are made to replace old, worn ones which have become too fragile to parade. This very special service remains an important part of the cathedral's calendar and George liaises closely with the cathedral's Dean and Chapter to make sure that things run smoothly. Understandably, the service is always well attended.

Different bands are chosen each year to take part in the service, although they are generally led by the Durham Miners' Association Band, formerly known as the NUM North-East Area Band, which, as George says, "knows the ropes". Only six bands at most are admitted to the cathedral, accompanied by the banners. Each band marches in, passing down the central aisle, playing an appropriately solemn piece, and when the service is over marches out to a jaunty air. A maximum of three bands accompanies the hymns because of the cathedral's acoustics.

The cathedral contains a chapel dedicated to the *Durham Light Infantry* (DLI), complete with colours from the regiment's campaigns – large numbers of the county's miners served in this regiment. George felt that the cathedral's existing miners' memorial – a dark, ornate fireplace – was not perhaps the most beautiful tribute to those who campaigned in the coal mines of the county to win a war against underground dangers. He believed that a miners' banner would be a fitting additional tribute and more colourful.

After much thought and discussion, the Dean & Chapter agreed to his request and today the Haswell Colliery lodge banner is displayed on a wall of the South Transept, opposite the DLI Chapel. It bears a slightly altered quotation from Hebrews in the New Testament, "They being dead yet speaketh". This is a reference to three union pioneers depicted on the banner: William Crawford, Tommy Ramsay and Alexander McDonald, of whom we will hear more later.

The memorial fireplace is, of course, retained, and next to it, below a pit lamp, is the Miners' Book of Remembrance, which lists, colliery-by-colliery, numerous men and boys who have lost their lives in the Durham pits. The fireplace bears an inscription which includes the words: "Remember before God the Durham Miners who have given their lives in the pits of this county and those who work in darkness and danger in those pits today."

The Gala Day

The Gala begins with miners from the various union lodges and their banners, families and friends assembling at various points in Durham, with the leading groups starting off the parade from the miners' headquarters,

Red Hill, which is located near the city's East Coast railway line. The other contingents join the parade close to Red Hill near the County Hospital, in the Market Place and at the New Elvet junction with Old Elvet, next to the County Hotel.

The bands, a considerable number of which now come from beyond the Durham coalfield, including Yorkshire, march with the lodge banners through the streets of the city centre, reaching the County Hotel where the guest speakers for the day and other leading figures stand on the hotel balcony. Each band pauses to play for the speakers, before moving off along Old Elvet towards the former racecourse, where the speeches take place and where a funfair, stalls and entertainment are provided.

Band and banners passing the County Hotel
Photo by John Attle

George Robson tells of the way things have changed over the years. "In former times the bands did not always play in front of the balcony, but simply marched past. Now, with them all pausing, it can take four and a half hours or more for the entire parade to reach the old racecourse".

When the lodge contingents have all passed, the Mayor of Durham, often in full ceremonial dress, leads the procession of DMA officers, speakers and other guests from the County Hotel to the racecourse platform. He or she is accompanied by a traditional bodyguard complete with ceremonial weaponry. Immediately before the speeches, **Robert Saint's** famed miners' anthem, *Gresford*, is played in front of the platform by a chosen band. The noise of the crowd respectfully subsides. Saint was a miner at Hebburn Colliery until its closure in 1931 and became conductor of the Harton Colliery Band of South Shields. He composed *Gresford* to commemorate the 266 men and boys who died in a disaster at Gresford Colliery, near Wrexham, North Wales, in 1934. His majestic and moving 'hymn', created in 1936, is now regarded as a classic in the repertoire of miners' brass bands. The 'hymn' had no words when it was composed, although some time later lyrics were written for the tune. They are rarely heard, and it is arguable that this 'song without words' speaks volumes.

After the performance of this beautiful piece, the Mayor welcomes the men, women and children of the mining communities to the city. The traditionally-dressed bodyguards stand in position in front of the platform. The speeches on the racecourse have always been an important feature of the day. Many renowned Labour politicians and trade union leaders have addressed the Gala crowds. The list of names includes ardent socialists such as Keir Hardie, A.J. Cook, George Lansbury, Aneurin Bevan, Hugh Dalton, Emanuel Shinwell, Sir Stafford Cripps, Michael Foot, Tony Benn, Arthur Scargill and Dennis Skinner.

The 1946 Gala saw Prime Minister Clement Attlee, Chancellor of the Exchequer Hugh Dalton and Minister of Health Aneurin Bevan on the speakers' platform – a prestigious line-up which marked a high tide for Labour. They were joined by Ebby Edwards, a Northumberland miner who had risen to become General Secretary of the NUM. In addition to Attlee, three other Labour prime ministers have spoken at the event – Ramsay MacDonald, Harold Wilson and James Callaghan.

The first woman to speak from the platform was birth control campaigner and socialist Annie Besant, in 1876. Mrs Besant, a supporter of Irish home rule, addressed the Big Meeting again in 1884. Other women guest speakers have included Ellen Wilkinson, the North East MP who championed the cause of the unemployed Jarrow marchers, Margaret Bondfield, who in 1929 became the first woman Cabinet minister, and Jennie Lee and Barbara Castle, both of whom served as ministers in Labour governments.

Perhaps the most unusual guest was Prince Peter Kropotkin, the Russian anarchist communist, who spoke in 1882. Of aristocratic birth, Kropotkin led a varied and extraordinary life – as a boy he was a member of the élite Corps of Pages at the court of the Tsar, he served in the Russian army in Siberia, became a distinguished geographer and later escaped from imprisonment in St Petersburg. He believed in the concept of co-operation without government control as the ideal for society. Kropotkin's fellow guests on this occasion included Joseph Cowan, the radical Liberal MP for Newcastle and one of the city's leading newspaper proprietors.

MUSICAL MORNINGS

On the morning of the Big Meeting, lodge members, accompanied by their families, friends and well-wishers, traditionally parade their banner around their colliery village or town. In former years, they were generally accompanied by the local colliery brass band, but, as mentioned earlier, today the band is sometimes brought from outside the locality, since many local groups were disbanded after the collieries closed.

The parading of the banner and band takes place at a relatively early hour. The musicians march through the streets, perhaps pausing to play outside the community's row of Aged Miners' Homes and at other significant points on their route, such as the site of the former mine or the welfare hall. Eventually, they set off for Durham, by coach or rail, and in earlier years, if the colliery village was situated close to Durham, the miners and their families, accompanied by the band and banner, simply marched all the way from home into the city.

Joining the parade at agreed points, the lodge parties and families march through the city centre behind their vibrant standards. Sometimes, a group of women, perhaps accompanied by men, will link arms and dance in sheer delight in front of the banner as they move along the crowded, narrow streets. A considerable number of people wear fancy dress in keeping with the fun side of the occasion. The atmosphere is always good humoured.

Today, onlookers frequently applaud the former miners; their way of life has been destroyed but in this heart-stirring parade their spirit lives on, and they are given recognition for being men who faced danger every day of their working lives underground. The spirit of their communities is alive too, and their families and friends display a strong pride in the traditions of the Gala.

On reaching the old racecourse each lodge ties or rests its banner against the perimeter fence of the site, with the instruments of their bands generally placed in front. A riot of colour thus borders the Gala field.

After the speeches and the cathedral service, the banners and bands gradually depart the racecourse, once more moving through the streets of central Durham, which are thronged with people in celebratory mood. The bands again play to the crowds and are always well received. Brass music finds a wide audience at the Big Meeting, providing a glorious, nostalgic soundtrack to the day.

On the return of the lodge parties to their communities, the bands may well once more strike up as the banners are paraded through their local streets in a fitting epilogue to the day's proceedings.

Jack Fletcher .... a miner's son remembers.

Schoolteacher Jack Fletcher of Chopwell is the son of a miner. His grandfather, Harry Bolton, *right,* was leader of the Chopwell Colliery miners during one of the longest disputes to grip the coalfield, the *Great Lockout* of 1926. The miners were fighting demands by the employers for wage reductions and longer hours. The men of Chopwell were particularly militant in resisting these demands, and the village was dubbed 'Little Moscow', although this pejorative description was unfair because its

Photo courtesy of Jack Fletcher

miners were more likely to be democratic socialists than communists, and many attended church, including Jack's grandfather, who was a Methodist. Harry Bolton served as a Durham County Councillor for many years and was the council's chairman for a period in the 1930s.

In fairness to the critics, Chopwell union lodge banner carries portraits of communists Marx and Lenin and socialist Keir Hardie. The pictures of Marx and Lenin were first painted on the standard in the early 1920s at a time when the miners were unaware of the ruthless nature of the Bolshevik regime in Russia. The banner bears a quotation from a Walt Whitman poem: "We take up the task eternal, the burden and the lesson. Pioneers! Oh! Pioneers".

These lines are particularly appropriate for trade unionists; Keir Hardie, Labour's greatest pioneer and perhaps the most famous miner of all, would undoubtedly have approved of the poet's words.

Jack Fletcher, who has lived in Chopwell all his life, writes of the Gala:

> *It always has been the highlight of the mining community's year. Speaking as a teacher, I regard it as a mixture of speech day and the end of term Christmas carol service; a mélange of sweet and sour; the serious and light-hearted; the sacred and profane. The Gala encapsulates the bold, optimistic sentiment which states, "We shall overcome".*
>
> *On that day, in mid-July, Durham belongs to the miners. Capture is complete; no quarter is given, but the atmosphere is forgiving, as the occupation of the city is benign and humane and will end in smiles at midnight. The ambience is still the same today, even though the mines are no more, for the Durham Miners' Gala has become a tradition, a piece of living history which has passed into folklore, like Morris dancing, strawberries and cream at Wimbledon and glasses of Pimms at the Henley Regatta. To appreciate what the Gala means you have to live it, experience it and surrender yourself to it.*

Jack remembers his impressions of the Chopwell 'Red Banner' as a boy:

> *The banner to me was an icon, bearing the images of Marx, Lenin and the kindly Keir Hardie, the last of whom my grandfather had known and briefly worked for.*

16

This was not an ordinary banner; this was a banner with a past, a banner with a history. It was acknowledged that my grandfather had taken its predecessor (the first one to bear the Marx and Lenin portraits) to Moscow. It was also known that this banner had been attacked and torn by some villagers antipathetic to it. But it had been resilient, like its supporters, and had survived. It had had its moments of triumph and also of grief, when black sashes tied to its canvas announced the death of those who had made the ultimate sacrifice in the winning of coal during the previous year.

He has clear memories of Gala Day:

In the cool, dew-laden morning, a group of young men could be seen placing the banner on big, long poles. Behind it followed a phalanx of men, women and children in their Sunday best. There was an air of expectation and suppressed excitement. Behind these were a group of musicians – remember the three famous interlocked Ms – mining, music and Methodism – their silver instruments glinting in a sun that would later test their stamina to the limit as the day wore on.

Suddenly sweet music filled the village streets and the procession moved on its way. Slowly it went around the village. The procession grew larger as doors and windows opened for people to get a better view and appreciate the music, now strident, now soft, until a climax was reached with the playing of the miners' hymn, Gresford, prompting a solemn calm and many a silent tear.

Thus the journey began. Music, music all the way, as these soldiers of the banner marched in step down the main street of Chopwell to Blackhall Mill. After that, up the hill to Hamsterley; through the village to High Westwood to the now non-existent railway station to wait for the train to Durham. Like the Pied Piper of Hamelin, this band of marchers increased, for these were purposeful, determined people looking forward to enjoying their business with pleasure.

Indian dancers enjoy the Gala spirit in Durham
Photo by Richard Smith

And what a sight met their eyes. The whole city was en fete. It was carnival time. The main streets were crammed with excited people. Their excitement was no longer suppressed; they roared with joy and enthusiasm as each banner went by. The atmosphere was electric, optimistic and purposeful.

The centre of attraction was the County Hotel, where, windows open, the Gala's guests of honour smiled, beamed and waved at the milling crowds below. In good-natured fashion they smiled back and saluted their guests.

Then there were the banners; banners of all colours and dazzling hues; a living, heaving kaleidoscope of whirling shades. These bore messages of solidarity and pictures of important national political figures. Some were historical, such as my grandfather's friend, miners' leader and Durham County Council chairman Peter Lee, or W.P. Roberts, the 'Pitman's Attorney'. Others included living political or trade union figures.

"Every mining community, every union lodge had its own banner. Some were old, some were new. They were being constantly created as the need arose. People were proud of them. They were also well looked after, and it must be acknowledged that there was great competition in this culture as to which banner was the most memorable and the most impressive.

To the great joy of those playing in Chopwell Silver Band, those tired but determined men parading the banner and those resilient souls who had set out from Chopwell early that July morning, there was no doubt as to which made the greatest impact on the crowd. There never had been any doubt as to which had been the most impressive banner. It had always been that way.

It had become tradition that at a particular time during the procession of banners through Durham City a tiny whisper would grow and grow until it became a mighty chorus; then a shout, 'There's the Chopwell banner!' And a huge cheer would arise. Then the clapping would begin and the cheering grow ever louder as Marx, Lenin and old Keir Hardie swept by.

Portrait of Keir Hardie on West Sleekburn banner

Jack points out that, ironically, each new Marx and Lenin banner is blessed by the Bishop in the cathedral, as any other. The images of these two luminaries of communism are carried into a place dedicated to a religion which they viewed as the "opium of the people". However, it is the portrait of Keir Hardie that is accorded central place on Chopwell's standard, and Jack feels that Hardie's picture redeems the banner. This renowned socialist believed in Christianity as well as democracy. Jack comments with dry humour, "Did all this mean that Chopwell people were not heathens after all?"

TO THE RACECOURSE

We arrive in Durham early on a cloudy morning in July 2007, to experience the 123rd Gala. The event's friendly organiser, George Robson, from whom we heard earlier in this book (see page 6), greets us at Red Hill where already, just after 8am, former miners and other trade unionists are assembling their banners in the grounds, and various bands are gathering.

Red Hill was opened in 1915 and was paid for by miners' contributions. It is an impressive building with a red and buff stone façade. The roof is crowned by a small dome and another dome sits on top of its fine entrance porch. Its gardens feature imposing statues of leading union pioneers, including William Crawford. These flank the driveway, as if gazing down upon the proceedings. Smaller statues of miners with picks adorn the pillars of the entrance gates.

The Red Hill gatehouse is a hive of activity – it is the office of Durham Colliery Mechanics. The affable **Jim Perry**, administrator of the Mechanics, talks to us about the organisation and proudly shows us its banner which has just been attached to the poles. It bears the motto, "The past we inherit, the future we build." In the lane outside the gates, Flass Street, the NUM North-East Area Band is already assembling, with the area banner held high behind them. They are to lead the march to the old racecourse, the first of an 'army' of colourful bands and banners which for the next four or more hours will tread through the streets of the venerable old city.

A gate pillar at Red Hill
Photo by Richard Smith

Behind them, a group of men from the *Bevin Boys Association* gather to take their place as second in the parade. They hold a green banner. We talked to a couple of these wartime miners, some of whom have journeyed from as far as the South Coast to be here, a pilgrimage to Durham they make each year. By now senior citizens, they clearly remember with affection their days in the mines, where they experienced an unsurpassed comradeship. Now, all these years later, they are here, preparing to march as the city begins to stir from sleep.

Suddenly, and seemingly unannounced, the bass drum of the Area Band sounds out with a loud pounding and then the other musicians raise their brass instruments to their lips. The sounds of cornets, baritone and tenor horns, euphoniums, trombones and tubas carry on the air down towards the city centre. The march has started. We join the group behind the Area banner, thrilled by the occasion.

It is an extraordinary moment. As we march, with the banner fluttering in the wind, our feelings are almost impossible to describe. We are taking part in an event which captures the spirit of the miners and their communities as no other; it is a privilege to be here, stepping out along these historic streets where generations of pitmen have stepped before us to show their solidarity and to express their humanitarian values.

One side of the area banner depicts Red Hill, Durham Cathedral, the Tyne Bridge and St Nicholas' Cathedral in Newcastle – County Durham and Northumberland united – together with roundel portraits of pioneering miners' union leaders Tommy Hepburn and Martin Jude and images of safety lamps. The motto reads: "United we stand – divided we fall". The standard is carried by Venture Scouts.

In this extraordinary parade there is a strong feeling of historical continuity. The miners are once more marching into Durham, following in the footsteps of their ancestors who with banners held proudly aloft trod this way over many decades to press for their 'reets'. As we enter central Durham crowds are already starting to form to watch the parade. In North Road, we pass the old Miners' Hall, completed in 1875, which served as the DMA headquarters until the opening of Red Hill.

The band marches confidently on, playing a stirring melody. We cross Framwellgate Bridge and the sun breaks through the clouds, its light streaming on to the silvery waters of the River Wear as if welcoming the miners to the city. The cathedral and castle, high above us, seem to join in the chorus of warm greetings.

The band reaches the Market Place in the city centre, presided over, in a touch of irony, by the equestrian statue of the 3rd Marquess of Londonderry in military uniform, *right,* a County Durham coal owner who opposed the pitmen's trade unions and the appointment of safety inspectors for mines. But it is the miners and their Gala which hold the attention of the already thickening crowds, not the Marquess. At this point, onlookers applaud to show their affection and high regard for the men from the pits.

Photo by Richard Smith

Soon we are crossing Elvet Bridge. A glance behind shows that we have been joined by other bands and banners. Standing out, behind the Bevin Boys, is the Craghead Lodge banner with its colourful yellow background, which bears portraits of 'Three Men of Merit' – Clement Attlee, Aneurin Bevan and Arthur Horner (a former leader of the NUM). Beyond the bridge lies the historic thoroughfare of Old Elvet. In time-honoured fashion, the Area Band stops in front of the County Hotel where the speakers and union leaders stand on the balcony, smiling down on the marchers. The musicians turn and play a jazzy piece for the balcony party. It is well received.

24

The Dawdon Lodge standard moves on from the County Hotel
Photo by John Attle

Then, up Old Elvet we march, the band playing tirelessly. Suddenly we veer to the left and pass down a sloping driveway to the beautifully green expanse of the old racecourse which lies pristine before us. Dotting the edges of the field are numerous tents, stalls and fairground rides. All is ready for the day's proceedings. It is not long before other bands and banners appear at the top of the slope. They are indeed like an army coming to the field, but a friendly, peaceful army with messages of togetherness and fraternity.

The procession of lodges takes several hours to pass down on to the racecourse. Among the first after the Area group are **Craghead** and **Springwell**. The Springwell banner carries the message, "Unity is Strength". Also early on the field is the handsome scarlet banner of **Wheatley Hill Lodge** bearing the unmistakable portrait of miners' leader Peter Lee who became chairman of Durham County Council and whose name lives on in the town of Peterlee. The other side features a biblical scene with the quotation, "Suffer the little children to come unto me".

Silksworth's banner carries a pithead scene, complete with winding wheels; **Esh Winning's** features the message, "All men are brethren" with a painting of a pitman and manager shaking hands; **East Hetton's**, generally known as **Kelloe**, depicts the Good Samaritan with the parable's message: "Go thou and do likewise." The **Murton Lodge** banner bears a socialist motto, "Production for use, not for profit". The other side carries a large portrait of Tommy Hepburn.

Conishead Priory
Ulverston

Photo by John Armagh

Several banners show Durham Cathedral and **Conishead Priory**, a former convalescent home for injured or sick miners, as well as various groups of Aged Miners' Homes. One example is that of **Vane Tempest**, which features the cathedral. Preceded by a red-coated band and followed by a **Fire Brigades Union** banner, Vane Tempest's standard billows in the wind until at one moment it flaps almost horizontally. With difficulty, we are able to discern that the reverse side depicts a bird's eye view of the colliery.

As the bands reach the field, we note that a large number of the players are aged under twenty, even though this is taking place in a coalfield where every deep mine has been closed. It seems that the ethos of the miners and their communities cannot be erased by government policy or decree.

As well as those representing the miners' lodges, there are banners from other trade unions which have come to show their solidarity with the pitmen. Taking their place in the line too, are the standards of the **Durham Aged Mineworkers' Homes Association**, bearing the portraits of association pioneers **John Wilson** and **Joseph Hopper**, and of **Thompsons Solicitors**, which carries a painting of 'Pitman's Attorney', **W.P. Roberts.**

Meanwhile, the racecourse has been filling up with happy people of all ages. Fun and solidarity are mingled. The funfair rides and stalls seem to be doing a good trade. Eventually, we can hear the stirring sound of a band playing *Gresford* and the speakers and other guests have assembled on the platform near the centre of the field.

At 3pm, the Miners' Festival Service begins in Durham Cathedral; the link between the pitmen and the cathedral remains strong. A senior cleric is on Palace Green to welcome the three bands and four banners chosen for the year. Two of the banners are new and are therefore to be dedicated by the Bishop; they are those of **Greenside** and **Deaf Hill**. The Greenside banner is accompanied by a tall miner in a pit helmet, *right*, who is clearly enjoying every moment of the occasion.

Photo by Richard Smith

27

We join the congregation. The service is packed with people, so it's difficult to find a vacant seat. The Bishop of Durham, the Rt Rev Dr Tom Wright, the Dean, The Very Rev Michael Sadgrove, and other clerics stand at the head of the nave, awaiting the banners. Then, muffled notes are heard which grow louder. The NUM North East Area Band enters through the main door of the cathedral and proceeds slowly up the aisle, playing softly a composition of great serenity, followed closely by their banner and the Deaf Hill banner. Afterwards, the two other bands and standards enter, again playing reverently. The Bishop dedicates and blesses the new banners in a service which enthralls everyone there. After the dedication, the Area band plays *Gresford,* an anthem that has frequently punctuated the day. The choir sings a setting of the bible verses and the Call to Remembrance inscribed on the cathedral's Miners' Memorial.

The sermon is delivered by the Rev Canon Dr David Kennedy, now Vice-Dean of the cathedral, who was brought up in South Shields and recalls the pits of his home area, **Harton** and **Westoe**. He tells the congregation that as a child, from his bedroom window he could see the pithead of Harton and the massive tower of the Westoe mine. He stresses the spirit of pride in the former mining communities of County Durham, which has outlived the closures. He describes the place of worship in which the congregation is assembled as the 'Miners' Cathedral'.

Canon David Kennedy
with the Miners' Memorial Lamp
Photo by Tom Yellowley

The sermon is a moving one:

The mines, the shipyards, the railways — it is remarkable that in a single generation we have seen almost everything go. The industries which formed County Durham culture, that gave rise to so many of our communities, that provided stability and identity, that guaranteed work, are now a memory, even if a cherished memory.

And how cherished — just think of today's banners. The Springwell banner: Springwell Colliery was opened in 1826 and closed in 1932, that's 75 years ago, but it is remembered, a colliery that in those dangerous days suffered three explosions, in 1833, 1837 and 1869, losing over 80 men and boys. Washington F Colliery: opened in 1777 and continuing for almost 200 years until its closure in 1968, when it employed 1,300 men. Deaf Hill Colliery: opened in 1877, and closing in 1967, still employing 600 men when it closed. Greenside Colliery: opened in the 1880s and closed in 1966, at its height in the 1930s employing 1,100 men and still some 500 when it closed. Thousands and thousands of people employed in this industry over many generations.

And I find, as I have talked to various people in preparing this sermon, that there are such a strange mixture of emotions in our villages and towns that have been formed by mining. It's a bit like when someone dies. Sometimes, it's a good death, when someone has lived a long life, has had a good life, and yes, there is the pain of parting, but we know that that person's life has run its course and we say 'thank you'. But sometimes, it's a cruel death, a premature death, where there is tragedy, and hurt, and sometimes we feel betrayed and let down. So, for the collieries: some had run their course, and were exhausted, and we knew that their day had come, and new jobs were found, even if that meant moving to new areas. But others, well, they were simply closed, without any regard for what would happen to their communities, or where new jobs would come from, or how community life might be sustained. And some of our communities still feel that – the merciless dismantling of a whole way of life, and promises of regeneration that perhaps in places were only partly kept. And some communities still have their stories of loss – I began my ministry in Spennymoor, and every time I did a burial in York Hill Cemetery, I passed the memorial to the 36 men and youths, some of them only 16, who died in the Tudhoe Colliery explosion in April, 1882.

But, whatever the story of your community, whatever emotions we bring to this service, the reason why Durham Big Meeting has just refused to die, is because we also have a tremendous sense of pride; pride in our communities, pride in our culture, pride in our history. Because there is something in the bloodstream of County Durham people that shouts 'never say die'; that fought the demolition of the category D villages in the 70s and 80s, that takes a pride in friendliness and neighbourliness, that wants the best for our children and young people, that wants to go on telling its stories and remembering the tradition of hard and dangerous work, of earning a decent living.

And signs of that 'never say die' spirit are seen in the procession of new banners dedicated by the Bishop year by year in this cathedral, by the brass bands which are such an important part of every Big Meeting, and the fact that people still make their pilgrimage, not only for the Big Meeting but throughout the year, to this cathedral, the Miners' Cathedral, to see the Miners' Memorial and the Book of Remembrance and Miner's Lamp, and the Haswell Lodge banner, which dates from 1893, permanently displayed in the South Transept to my left.

Towards the end of his sermon, Canon Kennedy tells the congregation,

I began with a view from the bedroom window of my childhood: the mines, the railways, the shipyards. All gone; certainly the mines, almost all the shipyards, and now there's only a mere shadow of the industrial railways. Houses now stand on the old playing fields of the North East Railway Company and on the sites of Harton and Westoe collieries. But I stand this afternoon with a more noble view than I had back then as a child: I see today the people of the County Durham communities, formed by coal mining, standing in a holy place, as people of faith, people of hope, people of resurrection.

The collection is for the Durham Aged Mineworkers' Homes Association Residents' Social and Welfare Fund and the work of the cathedral. At the end of the service, the bands and banners march out to lively tunes and the congregation begins clapping in time, giving them a rousing send-off. The hallowed walls of the great cathedral are filled with the spirit of the pitmen. The Bishop, Dean and other clerics are delighted with the sheer happiness and warmth which surround them in 'The Miners' Cathedral'. As we leave, we make a point of pausing at the Miners' Memorial and Book of Remembrance. A light shines from the pit lamp above the book.

The congregation begins to file out, and yet again we are reminded of the friendly links between the cathedral and the pitmen. As we have seen, Bishop Westcott began those links in 1892 and showed great concern for the miners' welfare, earning the title 'The Miners' Bishop'. A photograph of him is among the pictures which take pride of place on the walls of the Record Room at Red Hill.

Miners' Book of Remembrance
Courtesy Dean & Chapter

More Miners' Bishops

Another Bishop of Durham, **Handley Moule**, went to the pithead immediately after the West Stanley Colliery disaster of 1909, in which 168 men and boys lost their lives, and visited the homes of families bereaved by the tragedy. He had great sympathy for the pitmen and even penned a miners' hymn. Moule might well be regarded as the Second Miners' Bishop.

But the relationship between the Durham miners and the Anglican Church had a low amid its more usual highs. At the 1925 Big Meeting the Dean of Durham, **James Welldon**, was nearly pushed into the River Wear by a number of people who had apparently mistaken him for the Bishop of Durham, **Dr Herbert Hensley Henson**. This particular bishop was strongly independent-minded and forthright in speaking out. Rightly or wrongly, he had gained a reputation for holding opinions on political and social issues, including strikes, which conflicted with those of the miners. His complex views were easily misunderstood, and feelings were running high at this time because of unemployment among the miners. Despite all the commotion, Henson was not unsympathetic to the miners, as many apparently believed; his opinions could not easily be pigeon-holed.

Moments before the incident Dean Welldon was exchanging friendly greetings and joking with miners at the Gala where he was due to speak on the subject of temperance; not perhaps the most popular cause on Gala day. Welldon was a very tall man and Bishop Henson was very short, but despite the difference in height – and girth – Dean Welldon, in clerical attire, was seemingly mistaken for the bishop. He was pushed and jostled towards the river, with some people shouting that he should be "hoyed" in. Luckily, a motor boat drew up alongside the bank and he was able to board it. According to one version of the story, the Dean was almost knee deep in water before he was rescued. The episode occurred while the speeches were still in progress. Soon afterwards Dean Welldon appeared in the pulpit at the cathedral before the Gala service congregation of miners and their families. The kindly Dean appealed for more funds to be given to the Aged Miners' Homes.

The Miners' Memorial in Durham Cathedral was dedicated by Bishop **Alwyn Williams** in 1947. The warm relationship between the cathedral and the miners had by this time been cemented. Four years later, Dr Williams went to the pithead following the Easington disaster of 1951; he might be called the Third Miners' Bishop. The line of bishops who were associated with the pitmen continued. The Fourth was **Ian Ramsey**, enthroned in 1966, who made it clear that he, too, felt a strong concern for the miners and their communities. In 1971 he was one of the guest speakers at the Gala. On this occasion, Bishop Ramsey expressed his approval for the way the Durham miners and their union handled industrial disputes.

He declared that their record on the conduct of pay claims was a "shining example" to other industries. On the speakers' platform with him were TUC general secretary Vic Feather and Baroness Lee of Asheridge, better known as Jennie Lee.

The Fifth Miners' Bishop was **Dr David Jenkins**, enthroned in 1984, who spoke out at the height of the Great Strike of 1984-85 in which the miners fought against mass pit closures. Bishop Jenkins tried to encourage a humane settlement of the dispute. He declared that the "the miners must not be defeated", pointing out that the government under Prime Minister Margaret Thatcher seemed determined to achieve their defeat.

"The cost of hope in our society and in our politics is a responsible readiness for compromise," he said. He spoke of the desperation of the miners for the welfare and future of their communities. This had driven them to the action they were now taking. He stated that no one should forget what it meant to be part of a community centred on a mine or works when that mine or works closed. "It is death, depression and desolation," he declared. "A society which seeks economic progress for material ends must not indifferently exact such human suffering from some for the sake of the affluence of others."

Turning to the government under Prime Minister Margaret Thatcher, Bishop Jenkins said they seemed to be indifferent to "poverty and powerlessness". Their financial policies had consistently improved the lot of the already better off. He added that the government's answer to civil unrest seemed to be to make the means of suppression more efficient, while ignoring or playing down the causes. In speaking out during this troubled period Bishop Jenkins was following a tradition of concern for the miners and their families stretching back to Bishop Westcott in Victorian times. The warm relationship between the Durham pitmen and the cathedral lives on.

PROUD STANDARDS

The ideas for banner designs were supplied by the miners' lodges or were selected by the lodges from a manufacturers' catalogue of traditional themes and mottoes. However, a lodge might suggest alterations or additions to a traditional theme or motto to render its banner more distinctive.

Today, traditional themes are still often adhered to on one side of a banner, but new themes and images – sometimes suggested by local schoolchildren – are frequently selected for the other side. These ideas are then sent to the manufacturer.

In some instances, both sides feature entirely new themes, and in the case of a few banner groups the banner is made by members of the group or by professional North East artists and crafts people. Thornley's new standard is one example.

PROUD STANDARDS

The Messages of Banners

The brightly-painted lodge banners of the DMA and NUM are central to the Big Meeting; they are both moving and inspiring. Without them, the Gala would not be the Gala. Speeches have often made headlines, but to the majority of people the most inspiring feature of the Big Meeting is the wonderful parade of colourful banners and brass bands. The mottoes on the banners express heartfelt humanitarian values; perhaps modern Britain has too often strayed from these sound and decent principles. Throughout the coalfield, community banner groups have been formed to keep the tradition of these very special standards alive; former miners, their families and friends have rallied round to make sure that new banners are produced when needed and old ones preserved. These extraordinary icons of mining trade unionism are an extremely important part of the heritage of the pit communities, and each represents an entire community as much as it does its union lodge.

The Heritage Lottery Fund frequently helps with the substantial cost of providing new banners and funds are also raised by the groups themselves, with much of the support coming from the pit communities. In past years, before the Heritage Lottery Fund was set up, a lodge unable to afford its own banner might be given the banner of a recently closed colliery; the name of the new lodge was then painted over the old. But many veteran standards have been lost in the mists of time, their whereabouts a mystery. However, occasionally an old standard is discovered tucked away in an unexpected corner. For example, one 'lost' banner was found in the rafters of a pigeon cree.

The craftsmanship embodied in these standards is not to be under-estimated. The most prominent of the early banner makers was *George*

Tutill of London, a firm whose talented artistry and craftsmanship in silk was renowned in union circles. Later, the Tutill business was reborn when it moved to Chesham in Buckinghamshire following damage to its London premises during a Second World War bombing raid. Another well-known maker, *Turtle & Pearce*, based in London, carved out a fine reputation, too. Both of these businesses are still in existence and are part of the *Flagmakers Group*, their products including flags as well as banners, bunting and flagpoles. *Chippenham Designs*, of Overstrand, Norfolk, is also an important manufacturer in the banner market and has been responsible for many of the new standards which appear each year at the Festival Service.

To be selected to help carry the lodge standard was always a great honour for any pitman. A team of six was needed for the task: two men holding the poles using cupped harnesses and four to grip the guide ropes needed to steady the banner, particularly in windy conditions.

A banner carrier with the Lumley 6th Lodge standard
Photo by Richard Smith

Jim Wilson, of Usworth, Washington, worked in the pits of the Durham coalfield for 30 years. He served at the Glebe, Usworth, Boldon and Wearmouth collieries and did his training for the coalface at Westoe. Jim writes:

The first time I went with the Glebe was in 1967. I'd got my Durham money off the union in my pocket. I think it was only £2.10s but that was more than enough. Being only 15, I spent it all on the shows.

I was lucky enough to carry the Glebe banner out of Durham in the Centenary Gala. By this time most of the pits in Durham had closed along with the Glebe. There was only a handful left. What a sight it was to see the old banners with the cobwebs dusted off and the mass of people having one last dance along the street. The beauty of it, the banners being free once more.

I always think marching with the banner is akin to a guardsman trooping the colour. No guardsman could feel more pride.

His pride is understandable. The banners are rich in meaning; they symbolise the brotherhood of the miners – they are emblems of close friendships forged amid the dangers of working at the coal face. They also embody the spirit of the mining communities; emblazoned across their fabric are messages and pictures which reflect the history of the pitmen and their values.

Over the many years, the banners have also displayed poignant reminders of the great dangers faced by the pitmen. A tradition arose at the Gala of draping black crêpe across the top of a lodge banner if one or more miners from that lodge had been killed in an accident during the previous year. This solemn rite of black crêpe is still continued today if officials or other stalwarts of the lodge have passed away. Black crêpe was also frequently draped across the tops of banners during miners' funerals – another tradition which has endured. In this way, the men of the pits remember their fallen brothers.

Christianity has been a major influence in the mining villages and towns. Indeed, Methodist chapels are still to be found in most communities throughout the Durham coalfield, and many of the early union officials and leaders were Methodists, particularly of the Primitive denomination. It is therefore no surprise that these colourful standards frequently carry illustrations and quotations from the Bible.

Banners also proclaim the importance of trade unionism in protecting the miner and his family. In an industry where death, injury and illness were all too common, a strong trade union was vital to secure compensation and promote safety. Portraits of renowned union leaders, socialists and Labour politicians are therefore very much in evidence. For example, the North East Area NUM banner and those of six lodges display the portrait of Thomas Hepburn, who is regarded as the leading pioneer of mining trade unionism in the North East.

Thomas Hepburn

Born at Pelton in County Durham, Hepburn was an advocate of better education for miners and their children. In 1831, he led a strike in which the pitmen called for improved wages, a reduction in the long working hours, particularly for boys, and an end to the Tommy shops system. Tommy shops were stores owned or favoured by their employers. The men were forced to buy their food and other provisions from them and money was deducted from their wages to pay for the items.

The strike was a bitter one, but the miners eventually achieved a partial victory. The hours for boys were reduced to twelve, and it was agreed that the men and their families could buy their provisions from stores of their own choice. However, to what extent this agreement was honoured is hard to ascertain.

In 1832, the mine owners refused to employ men who were members of Hepburn's union and their comrades joined them in a strike in which they boycotted the hated annual contract known as the Bond. This contract bound them to work for their employer for a year on penalty of fines or imprisonment. But, as we have seen, their employer was under no obligation to give them work during this period.

The owners responded by evicting miners who were union members and their families from their colliery-owned cottages. Men from other parts of Britain, including Wales and Ireland, along with lead miners from the North Pennines, were brought in as blackleg labour and housed in the cottages. It is likely that many were unaware of the strike when they were signed on. It was a bitter dispute and by July 1832 the striking pitmen were beginning to drift back to work. These returning miners were forced to give up union membership as a condition of employment. Wage reductions followed.

Hepburn was refused work at the pits he applied to and was reduced to a state of destitution. However, after nearly two years the leader eventually obtained a job at Felling Colliery in Gateshead – but only on condition that he, too, gave up all union activity. He died in 1864 and is buried in

St Mary's Churchyard at Heworth, Gateshead, where North East miners pay tribute to him each year at a memorial service. Lodge banners are displayed inside the church for the occasion, and after the main service, the standards are taken to Hepburn's graveside and wreaths are laid as *Gresford* is played. In the same churchyard, a small obelisk commemorates 91 men and boys who died in the Felling Colliery disaster of 1812. The 92nd victim was never found.

A plaque on the Felling Disaster Memorial shows that boys as young as eight and ten years old were among the victims
Photo by Tom Yellowley

Another miner's hero represented on banners is **Tommy Ramsay**, whose memorial can be found in Blaydon Cemetery. He was a great recruiter for the DMA during its formative years and toured the pit communities with his crake (rattle), encouraging men to join and attend the meetings. Banners often recall the early struggles of the miners. One such is that of **Monkwearmouth Lodge** (often referred to as Wearmouth). One side of the banner depicts a courtroom scene. This commemorates the cancellation of the Bond at Monkwearmouth Colliery following a strike in 1869. Four miners accused of breaking their Bond by leaving their work were brilliantly defended by W.P. Roberts, the 'Pitman's Attorney'. The cancellation of the Bond at this pit was a catalyst which led to the formation of the Durham Miners' Association later that year. The motto is a quotation from The Bible, which reads, "Come let us reason together". It is a call for constructive negotiation as the way forward to resolve disputes.

Some versions of the Wearmouth banner depict on the other side a miner leaving home for the last time before his death at the pit, with his wife and children bidding him goodbye. The words poignantly read, "The last good morning". An adjacent illustration shows his wife as a widow, appearing before his employers. "We claim compensation," declares the inscription.

Trade unionism, with its fundamental message of the need for the miners to be united, is indeed one of the most abiding themes on the banners. The motto "Unity is Strength" and an illustration depicting the fable that a bundle of sticks is stronger than one stick on its own has often been featured. However, frequently buildings or places significant to the pitmen are illustrated. Favourites include groups of Aged Miners' Homes in the various communities, Durham Cathedral and Conishead Priory in Cumbria, once a convalescent home for injured or sick miners.

Among the politicians who have been represented was a prime minister who eventually fell dramatically from favour with the miners. Labour leader **Ramsay MacDonald** was a guest speaker at the Big Meeting on two occasions before the First World War and in the 1920s, but as Prime Minister in 1931 MacDonald decided to back cuts in public spending, including unemployment benefit. He formed a National Government with the Conservatives and Liberals to implement the cuts, all of which resulted in his portrait being removed from banners.

Derrik Scott, a former mining engineer of Springwell, recalls...

Derrik Scott, of Springwell worked in the pits for 36 years. He started at Usworth Colliery in 1950 at the age of twenty and became a miner at the face. His aim was to obtain a Manager's certificate and this he achieved in 1958, becoming an overman at Usworth, which meant that he was in charge of operations in a large section of the mine.

Gala veteran Derrik Scott at the site of Washington F Pit
Photo by Tom Yellowley

In 1960, Derrik took up a post as safety officer at Washington F Pit and stayed there until 1966 when he transferred to Westoe Colliery at South Shields, becoming a senior safety engineer. He served at Westoe for twenty years until his retirement in 1986.

Remarkably, Derrik has been going to the Big Meeting for over sixty years; he first attended the event at the age of three in 1933 with his father who was a miner at Usworth.

> *We travelled to the Gala by train. My mother told us that on my first attendance I and my younger brother fell asleep during the cathedral service. For weeks afterwards I kept asking my mother if I could go back to Durham and became quite insistent, so the Gala must have made a big impression on me even at that early age. My mother said I couldn't go again just yet. Why? I asked. Because there would be no bands and banners there until next year, she told me.*

In fact, he was taken to the event several times in the late 1930s and remembers that he and his brother sometimes ended up in the marquee for lost children after becoming separated from their parents in the huge crowds. Derrik has only missed one Gala since 1946 and it is clear he still regards the event as the highlight of the year. "The Big Meeting of 1946 sticks out in my mind," he says. "It was the first after the end of the Second World War. The colourful banners and bands were wonderful to see after the drabness of the wartime years." He adds: "My favourite banner is Sunnybrow's. It depicts the Good Samaritan on one side and on the other a widow with her children beside her husband's grave. The words read 'We succour the widow and orphans'. This made clear that the union was determined to look after the families of men killed working in the pits. The colours are beautiful."

Derrik tells of the sheer spontaneity, fun and enjoyment of the Big Meeting. "It's not all about politics and serious issues. Far from it." He remembers being in the group which accompanied the Usworth banner into the city at a Gala in the early 1960s. He was with his elder son. Afterwards, they accompanied the Washington F standard on the march-out. Derrik recalls:

> *Many people were heading for the station to catch trains home, but the crowds were so vast there was an impasse and the march came to a standstill. The band kept playing. They struck up a Spanish gypsy dance and the lodge chairman, a big man who weighed nearly twenty stone, got hold of two sticks of candy rock and put them on his head, pretending they were bull's horns. He became the bull and another man used his jacket to act the role of the toreador. It was hilarious. The crowds loved it.*

The impasse did eventually clear – perhaps the bull and toreador had something to do with it – and Derrik and his companions need not have worried. They caught their train. "There were plenty of trains in and out of Durham on Gala day. In fact, extra trains were laid on." Sometimes the fun would start even before the Big Meeting. He tells of a young timber leader at Washington F who was "as strong as an ox" and had the job of taking pit props to the coal faces:

> *In those days, a draw from a hat was held to determine which men would have the honour of carrying the lodge banner into Durham. There were over 1,000 miners at the pit, so a draw was essential. This young man's name came out of the hat, but one of the miners later joked that he did not believe the chosen lad was strong enough to help carry it. This resulted in the lad taking part in a fun test in which he had to carry a pit prop in a mock parade as if it was one of the banner poles. This took place underground. Needless to say, he passed the test.*

The miners contributed money each week from their wages towards a union lodge fund so that when the time for the Big Meeting came they would each receive a free railway ticket and a cash allowance for the day. All the Durham lodges did this.

> *A large part of the money often went on beer. It can't be denied that drinking was a major feature of the event. In fact, the pubs in Durham were open all day. It was jokingly said that by about 3pm the beer pumps were connected to the River Wear because the landlords had run out of supplies.*

But he makes clear that there was rarely any trouble, despite the many pints supped.

> *If there were any problems in the city, they normally happened in the evening after the vast majority of miners had gone home. Most pitmen were back in their communities by then and the Gala was over. And not every miner, of course, was a drinker. There were teetotallers among their ranks who still regularly turned out for the big day.*

Derrik's saddest memory is of the Easington lodge banner draped in black at the Big Meeting of 1951. It took place only a few weeks after the Easington Colliery disaster, which claimed the lives of 81 miners and two rescue workers.

> *I remember the banner arrived on the racecourse very late because large numbers of people in the crowds wanted to express their sympathies to the bereaved community and pay their respects to the departed. It was held up for hours. Almost immediately after reaching the field the lodge party and banner had to turn around*

and leave because the march-out had begun. I doubt they heard
any of the speeches.

Of the many speakers he has heard address the Gala crowds, Derrik views
Tony Benn as "consistently the best", and recalls that one year Mr Benn
delivered the sermon at the Miners' Festival Service.

Looking back at the pitmen's leaders, he particularly remembers **Sam
Watson**, the famed general secretary of the DMA who presided over the
record-crowd Gala days of the late 1940s and 1950s with a fatherly eye.
Sam, from Boldon Colliery, dedicated his life to the welfare of the Durham
pitmen and their families. A hard worker, he served as general secretary
for twenty seven years and was a great enthusiast for the Big Meeting. In
1961, the Sam Watson Rest Home, at Richmond, North Yorkshire, was
opened to provide holiday breaks for wives and widows of miners.

In 2000, Derrik, a lifelong Methodist, had the honour of helping to carry
the new Springwell lodge banner into the cathedral to be dedicated and
blessed by the Bishop. He took part in the ceremony as the representative
of the Springwell community, in which he has lived with his wife Mavis
for thirty seven years. "The Miners' Festival Service is wonderful. It should
be televised," he declares.

Bob Melvin of New Herrington

Bob Melvin worked as a miner at New Herrington Colliery, starting at the
pit in 1959 and leaving only when it closed in 1985. He was a leading
light in the formation of a miners' banner partnership at New Herrington.
In 2000, the latest lodge standard, replicating one of 1955, was unfurled
at the village's club by former president of the NUM Arthur Scargill. It

was taken to the Big Meeting for the first time that same year. The new banner had been largely financed by a grant from the Heritage Lottery Fund, with the rest of the money coming from fund-raising efforts in the community. It was made by Chippenham Designs.

This standard, and an earlier one of 1932, are displayed to the public, together with mining memorabilia items, on three days a week at the YMCA building at Herrington Burn. The latest banner, as its predecessor of 1955, carries portraits of Keir Hardie, Peter Lee and A.J. Cook. The words declare, "Men of the People". The reverse side depicts the DMA headquarters at Red Hill and its miners' memorial garden. The garden is a tribute to the victims of the Easington and Eppleton disasters. The motto reads, "For Peace and Freedom".

The 1932 banner carries lines from the Communist Manifesto: "Workers of all lands unite! You have nothing to lose but your chains, you have a world to win". A female figure symbolising Progress carries a flag labeled, "Emancipation of Labour" with miners and their families following her to a better life in the "Co-operative Commonwealth". The other side depicts Conishead Priory.

New Herrington Lodge of the DMA now organises an annual service in memory of all miners throughout the North East coalfield. "It's held in the open air on the site of the skip-winding shaft of New Herrington Colliery," says Bob. "The area is now a country park." Attendances at the service grow each year. After the event, a brass band entertains the congregation at the village club. Bob is delighted at the way support for the Gala has grown since the closure of all the Durham pits. "At one point we thought we were going to lose this priceless event."

Derek Gillum of Doxford Park, Sunderland, was a miner for twenty five years, serving at Silksworth, Seaham and Vane Tempest collieries. His father, grandfather and great grandfather were also County Durham pitmen and he still lives close to the site of the former Silksworth mine. Derek was once off work for more than a year after being injured on the coalface at Vane Tempest.

He told us that the funds for the latest Silksworth standard were raised entirely by the area's banner group without the aid of a Heritage Lottery grant. The banner was painted by Bearpark Co-operative Artists' Group and was first paraded at the 2005 Gala. One side shows the colliery and the other carries portraits of Keir Hardie, A.J. Cook and Peter Lee.

John Taylor was a miner at East Hetton (Kelloe) Colliery from 1977 to 1983. He then transferred to Easington Colliery where he stayed until the pit closed in 1992. He is custodian of the Kelloe lodge banner. One side of this standard shows the Good Samaritan, with the inscription "Go thou and do likewise", and the reverse depicts the widow of a miner and her child beside his grave. The words read, "For all who suffered". Also shown on this side is part of the Kelloe village memorial to victims of the Trimdon Grange Colliery disaster of 1882. An explosion at the mine led to the deaths of 74 men and boys. Twenty six of these came from Kelloe and are buried at the site of the memorial. The Trimdon Grange and Kelloe collieries were linked underground.

The latest banner, produced in 2006 by Chippenham Designs, was paid for by a Heritage Lottery Fund grant. John explains that the grant also financed restoration work on the memorial: the names of the miners who died had suffered from years of exposure to the elements; the money enabled them to be read clearly again.

Mike Syer is secretary of the **Bowburn Banner Group**; banners which have survived for many decades are always of great interest, and one of the oldest is that of Bowburn Lodge which is believed to be unique in the North East. Dating to 1920, it is the only banner known to depict an identifiable woman – First World War heroine Nurse **Edith Cavell**. Nurse Cavell, *left*, was executed by the German military in 1915; she had helped many Allied soldiers escape from Belgium while the country was under German occupation.

Mike, who is also a former councillor, makes it clear that today people can only speculate as to why the portrait of this courageous woman was painted on the standard. Perhaps it was simply because her humane actions and bravery were admired by the men of Bowburn Colliery; she was lauded after the war and was given what amounted to a state funeral.

A relatively large proportion of men from the village served in the Armed Forces during the First World War. It could be that Edith Cavell helped one of them to escape. We just don't know. There was a story that this banner had been made by the pit painter, a Mr Merrington, but this was disproved when it was 'discovered' in 2005 and found to be a genuine Tutill product, painted on silk. My own theory is that there was an earlier, home-made one, painted soon after Nurse Cavell was executed, and that the lodge commissioned a new banner from Tutill's after the war, with a copy of the original portrait.

The other side of this veteran standard carries a painting of DMA leader **John Wilson**, who was general secretary from 1896 to 1915. Wilson was also the first president of the Durham Aged Mineworkers' Homes Association and received an honorary degree from Durham University in recognition of his work in this field. In addition, he served as 'Liberal-Labour' MP for Mid Durham, remaining a Liberal and never joining the Labour Party.

The 1920 banner and another of 1959 carrying an illustration of the old racecourse on Gala day were restored with the aid of a Heritage Lottery Fund grant. The money also paid for the production of a *new* Bowburn banner. This carries an illustration of three of the Bowburn lodge standards and crowds in Old Elvet during the Gala parade. With a nostalgic but moving touch, the words read: "The March of Time." The reverse side carries the motto, "Together we'll hew our future from the past". The new banner first appeared at the Big Meeting in 2006.

The Edith Cavell standard was in very poor condition when the banner group acquired it; in fact, it consisted of two large fragments. They had been saved from oblivion by Arthur Moyes, author of *The Banner Book*, which is regarded as a classic volume by aficionados of the Durham miners' standards. Superb restoration work by paint conservator Jim Devenport at Northumbria University in Newcastle and by textile conservator Caroline Rendell brought the banner back to life. Also playing an important role were postgraduate student Sarah Maisey, who carried out research and paint analysis, and Norma Johnson who assisted with the restoration. The team's efforts proved a triumph.

Edith Cavell was not a prominent socialist or Labour politician, but she was accorded a place of honour by the pitmen of Bowburn – a lone woman amongst a host of men in the Durham miners' gallery of fame. Thanks to the restoration work she still looks out to us across the many years which have elapsed since her tragic end.

Nurse Edith Cavell on the restored
Bowburn Lodge banner
Photo by John Attle

MAGNIFICENT BRASS

The other essential ingredient of Durham Big Meeting is the dazzling array of brass bands. They are as fundamental to its success as the banners; the two elements are inseparable.

The vast majority of the present-day brass groups in the county are descended from miners' bands, with some, such as Easington, still proudly retaining the name "colliery" in their titles. However, after the closure of the pits, finance for these dedicated musical groups was no longer available from miners' union lodge contributions. Many bands accordingly sought sponsorship from other organisations, although they often retained strong support within their communities. Some became largely self-supporting, deriving a large part of their income from concerts.

Alan Cummings was a miner at Easington Colliery for thirty years, working there from the age of fifteen until the pit's closure in 1993. Today, he is secretary of the village's DMA lodge and president of **Easington Colliery Band**. The band can trace its origins to 1913 and there are still one or two former miners among its ranks. Pitmen's sons, daughters, and grandchildren are also members; these young people are vital for its future.

Alan makes it clear that concerts help the group to be partly self-supporting but other funds come from sponsorship and donations. It costs a considerable amount of money to keep the band going, particularly with the group entering national competitions. The band lies at the centre of the community, as does its banner. The latest Easington Colliery banner shows the village's Community Garden on one side and Easington Primary School on the other, with the motto "Education is our Future." Alan explains that this garden was laid out in memory of all those who worked at the colliery below and above ground, both men and women, and including all mineworkers who lost their lives or were injured. It is opposite the site of the pit. The band is based in the old colliery pay office.

"The Community Garden is a peaceful spot, even though it's by the road. I sometimes go there to reflect," he says. The garden features a pit wheel motif and its entrance gates are based on one of the lodge banners, including portraits in metalwork of Tommy Hepburn and a more recent miners' leader, Lawrence Daly. The village also has two fine memorials to the 81 miners and two rescue workers who lost their lives in the 1951 Easington Colliery disaster. Seventy two of the dead are buried side by side in a memorial garden at the centre of the village cemetery, known as the Garden of Remembrance. At one end of the garden is a relief sculpture of a miner, complete with helmet and carrying a safety lamp. Next to him is a large lump of coal surmounted by a cross. Flanking the relief are two coal-filled tubs on rails, and close to the relief is a coal cutter machine. At the other end of the garden is a relief depicting safety lamps, which faces the graves. Incorporated into the impressive tribute are sculptures of lamps and picks.

Alan Cummings,
Lodge Secretary
and
President of Easington Colliery Band
at the
Easington Colliery disaster memorial
in the village cemetery.

Photo by Tom Yellowley

The other memorial takes the form of an avenue of trees leading to Easington Colliery Welfare Park. Each tree represents one of the victims; the first was planted by a sixteen year old miner in 1952. Sited in the avenue is a large stone from the scene of the disaster which bears a memorial tablet urging passers by to "get understanding and promote goodwill in all things".

Like Derrick Scott, Alan told us about the 1951 Gala, which took place only a few weeks after the disaster. The Easington banner was held up in the parade for hours. "Many people wanted to touch and feel the cloth. I think it was their way of trying to get close to those who lost their lives." A long-serving miner, Alan recalls the unequalled "camaraderie and crack" of the colliery. His son, John, also worked at the pit. "John was only at the mine for four years, but my son says he would go back if he could".

Members of Craghead Colliery Band in their rehearsal room with musical director John Robson (seated). The Craghead Banner is on display. *Photo by Tom Yellowley*

The musical director of **Craghead Colliery Band** is former miner **John Robson**, of Herrington Burn. He worked at Eppleton and South Hetton collieries and was a member of Hetton Silver Prize Band for thirty-one years. John's instrument was tenor horn. Today's Craghead Colliery Band is the second to bear the title. The original group became the Reg Vardy Band, which sometimes takes part in the Gala. John explains that the present Craghead Colliery Band originated as the band of the **Sacriston** miners, but later moved its base to Craghead. A large number of the thirty or so musicians are young people, many of whom were trained to play by John and other senior members. Concerts provide a large proportion of the group's funds.

Their chosen music is wide-ranging in style, but tradition reigns immediately before the Big Meeting:

> *On Gala morning we play Gresford outside the Craghead community centre and then march with the banner to the working men's club close to the site of the former mine where we play Gresford again. Then we board the coach to Durham. On returning to the village, we play at the same spots.*

Other traditional pieces which are played by the band include *Death or Glory*, *Sons of The Brave*, *Imperial Echoes* and *The Middy*, but John indicates that it is always refreshing to perform something new. They try to play a different tune each year for the guests on the County Hotel balcony: in 2008, the choice was the theme music from *The Great Escape* and the year before it was *Zambesi*.

Billy Elliott, who lives at Fishburn, is accustomed to the inevitable jokes about his name being the same as the pit village boy depicted in the acclaimed film *Billy Elliot*. He is vice president of the highly successful **Fishburn Band** and secretary of its support group.

The band was formed by Fishburn Colliery union lodge officials in

1953-54 and miners from the pit joined. It was known in those days as Fishburn Colliery Welfare Band. Today, all the original pitmen musicians have passed away, but their spirit lives on in the present group. "Several of the current band members are the sons of miners," says Billy, who worked as a pitman for twenty-nine years, serving at Fishburn, East Hetton and Vane Tempest collieries.

Fishburn Band marches through the village on Gala morning 2007
Photo by Tony Griffiths

The Fishburn Band won the Scottish Open Championship in 2005 and in the following year represented the Northern Area at the Great Britain Brass Band Championships at the Royal Albert Hall. They achieved 12th place in competition with nineteen other highly accomplished groups. In 2000, they captured the top place in the Durham Brass Band League contest for the fifth year in succession. The musicians, who include a considerable number of young men and women, put in many hours of practice to gain such wonderful results. They rehearse two days a week and then nearly every day when a contest or other key event is coming up. Billy explains that the residents of Fishburn are great supporters and help with fund-raising efforts for instruments and other expenses. The band has also received grants from the Heritage Lottery Fund and the Foundation for Sport and the Arts.

It was Billy Elliott's father, George, who first conceived the idea of forming the band. George was a miner too; he was killed in an accident at Fishburn Colliery in the 1950s. He and Mick Terrans, who became leader of Durham County Council, were lodge officials and they were prime movers in launching this renowned musical group.

On the eve of the Gala, the Fishburn musicians play an annual free concert in the village's workingmen's club. Billy told us that this is a way of saying "thankyou" to all those who have supported them during the year. They also hold a free concert at Christmas.

The band parades around the village on the morning of Gala day, starting off at around 8am. They stop to play outside the Aged Miners' Homes and the homes of other elderly people. If a former miner has died during the year, they play *Gresford* outside his home for his widow or other members of his family. At the Big Meeting, Billy marches in front of the band with his granddaughter, Leonie, who is their mascot. This group of talented brass musicians is the pride of the village.

Not surprisingly, Billy's favourite standard is Fishburn's. The present one dates to 2000 and, like the previous banner (see next page), carries portraits of Keir Hardie, A.J. Cook and George Lansbury but also features a portrait of the late Mick Terrans, who did much work for the Fishburn community and, as we have seen, was a founder of the band. The motto on the reverse of the new banner reads, "The cause of labour is the hope of the world".

A veteran Fishburn banner
Photo by Jean Smith

Banners and bands stream down from Elvet Bridge
into Old Elvet during the 2006 Gala.
Photo by Stafford Linsley

Fishburn band and banner seen from the balcony of the County Hotel, 2007
Photo by Tony Griffiths

The Haswell Lodge banner of 1893 which is on display at Durham Cathedral
Photo by Derrik Scott

Two banners are carried up the aisle at the Miners' Festival Service, 2007
The NUM North East Area standard is in front
with the Deaf Hill Lodge banner following
Photo by Bob Bach

The Bishop of Durham, Tom Wright, and other senior clerics at the Miners' Festival Service, 2007
The Greenside banner shows a view of the pithead

Photo by John Attle

Young musicians with the Washington F Pit banner at the 2008 Gala
Photo by Richard Smith

Boldon Lodge banner on the racecourse at the Big Meeting, 1965
A portrait of Jack Lawson, top, is prominent
Photo by Stafford Linsley

Former miners, Norman Raine, left, and Bob Melvin
with the New Herrington banner at the Gala, 2009
Photo by Jean Smith

Banners at the graveside of pioneering miners' trade union leader Thomas Hepburn at the Hepburn Memorial Service at St Mary's Church, Heworth, Gateshead, 2008

Photo by Bob Herrick

Members of Craghead Colliery Band with conductor John Robson (seated)
in their rehearsal room
Photo by Tom Yellowley

Houghton-le-Spring Pipe Band with the Lumley 6th Lodge banner
crossing Elvet Bridge on the march-out at the 2009 Gala
Photo by Jean Smith

The new Handon Hold Colliery Lodge banner is carried out of Durham
following its dedication at the cathedral on Gala day 2008

Photo by Richard Smith

A band performs outside the County Hotel with the East Hetton (Kelloe) banner
Photo by John Attle

First to arrive, NUM North East Area Band, now Durham Miners' Association Band,
leads the parade onto the racecourse on Gala morning, 2007
Photo by Richard Smith

Musicians and banners on the racecourse at the 1969 Gala
Photo by Stafford Linsley

Unity message: The Trimdon Grange Colliery banner
Photo by Jean Smith

Today we may be strong and healthy,
But how soon there comes a change,
As we may learn from the explosion
That has been at Trimdon Grange.

From 'The Trimdon Grange Explosion' by Tommy Armstrong, Pitman Poet

NUM North East Area Band, now Durham Miners' Association Band, reaches the crossing of the nave and transepts at the 2007 Miners' Festival Service
Photo by Bob Bach

The new South Hetton banner, dedicated in 2009

Photo by Arnold Ellis

The Easington Lodge standard at the racecourse fence with band instruments in front, Gala 2009

Photo by Jean Smith

The Chopwell Lodge banner on parade in the village on Gala morning
Photo by Mick Tilley

Craghead 'Three Men of Merit' banner and band members in the 2008 Gala parade
Photo by Richard Smith

Members of Dobcross Silver Band with the new Boldon banner outside
Durham Cathedral before the 100th Miners' Festival Service, 2009
Photo by Jean Smith

Indian musicians entertain the Gala crowds on the racecourse
Photo by Tony Griffiths

Pipe band passing the County Hotel, Durham
Photo by Richard Smith

Northumberland Miners' Picnic at Attlee Park, Bedlington, late 1950s or early 1960s
Photo by Derrik Scott

A happy contingent with the Pegswood banner leaves Attlee Park
after the Miners' Picnic, late 1950s or early 1960s
Photo by Derrik Scott

Memorial statue to the thirteen miners who
died in the Woodhorn Colliery disaster,
13th August 1916
Photo by Tom Yellowley

Woodhorn Museum grounds during the
Miners' Picnic weekend, 2009
Photo by Richard Smith

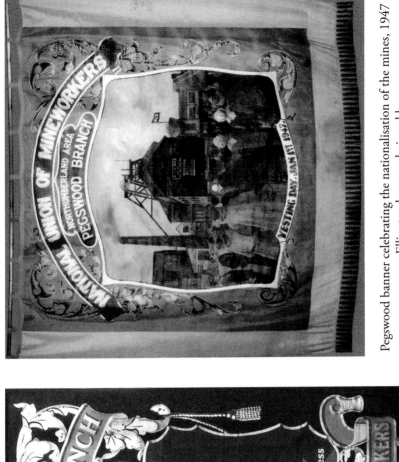

Pegswood banner celebrating the nationalisation of the mines, 1947
Ellington banner, designed by
famous Pitman Painter Oliver Kilbourn
Photos by Derrik Scott

Two banners photographed at the Picnic late 1950s early 1960s

Left, Hartford banner with a view of Hartford Hall, the injured miners' convalescence and rehabilitation home

Right, Netherton Colliery banner; the current whereabouts of these banners is unknown

Photos by Derrik Scott

Banners and wreaths at the Northumberland Miners' Memorial Service
in Holy Sepulchre Church, Ashington, 2009
Photo by Richard Smith

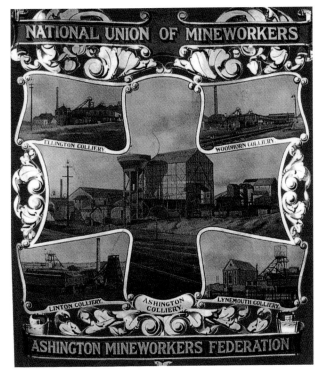

The NUM Ashington
Mineworkers' Federation
banner
*Photo by Derrik Scott,
late 1950s early 1960s*

Artist and principal Gala organiser George Robson in his studio at Red Hill, Durham
Photo by Tom Yellowley

George Robson's painting of the Murton banner with happy people on Gala day
Photo by George Robson

BANNERS IN THE AISLE

We arrive in Durham early on the morning of July 12th 2008 and join the Thornley Colliery party as they line up with their banners near the road junction below Red Hill. The 124th Gala parade is about to start. Yet there are no officials from the NUM directing the proceedings or issuing orders. This is not an over-controlled event and it never has been; the men, their families and their friends organise themselves in an informal way and things generally work out well. Spontaneity reigns, but the event is still essentially peaceful and orderly.

Billy Middleton, a stalwart of the new **Thornley** banner group, explains there are two main banners from the village this year – the new and the old. The new one is to be dedicated and blessed by the Bishop at this year's Miners' Festival Service. It carries a fine painting of the village's now demolished St Bartholomew's Church. The other side depicts Durham Cathedral and the Miners' Memorial Lamp. The men who lost their lives are never forgotten.

The paintings on the new banner are the work of artist Bob Ord, from Thornley, who was a churchwarden at St Bartholomew's. His excellent illustration of this much-loved church shows a plain but neat, well-proportioned building. Bob and Billy explain that the churchyard contains a memorial to around ninety of the pitmen who died working at Thornley Colliery.

The painting of the cathedral on the other side of this standard depicts this great ecclesiastical building lightly shrouded in mist. Billy Middleton tells the story of the German bomber planes which threatened the city during the Second World War. Before they could attack, a mist formed and shrouded the cathedral in a protective cloak "It was dubbed *St Cuthbert's Mist*," he says, adding that perhaps the mist on the banner is inspired by this story.

Billy, who was a blacksmith at Thornley and Easington collieries, informs us: "The old banner will be brought into the cathedral first, followed by the new. At the end of the service the new standard will go out first, with the old one following. This is traditional. But these days not every lodge has an old banner. Some have been lost and others are so badly worn or damaged they cannot be paraded".

With the colliery banners is a smaller one, made by the children of Thornley Primary School, with youngsters and parents in attendance. It features mining themes and adds further colour to the village's contribution.

Thornley Primary School Banner, Festival Service 2008
Photo by Richard Smith

The NUM North East Area Band (now renamed the Durham Miners' Association Band) leads the parade down from Red Hill, then come the men of the Bevin Boys' Association, with the Durham Colliery Mechanics taking third place in a line of banners and bands destined to grow longer and longer.

Immediately after the Durham Colliery Mechanics sweep past, the Thornley contingent join the march as fourth group in the line, with their banners flapping in the wind and the red-coated men and women of the Area Band providing a stirring, emotion-filled accompaniment of brass harmonies. The spirit of the miners and their communities is expressed to perfection in this wonderful music, equalled only by the colourful images and principled mottoes on their banners. People line the narrow streets, clapping and cheering the marchers as they do every year.

We parade into central Durham behind the old Thornley banner, which is covered in transparent plastic to protect it from further wear and tear. Billy explains that this is the last time the veteran standard will be carried into the city. Afterwards it will be 'retired'.

The banner was made in 1953 and small tears are visible near its top – a sure sign of old age. One side depicts the Greenwood Aged Miners Homes in Thornley and the other shows a recreation ground, above which are the words "Peace and Prosperity". The recreation ground features people of varying age groups enjoying sports and games: a young couple are carrying tennis racquets, men are playing football in the distance and a group of girls are skipping with a rope. The vision is one of a healthy, happy life to which the miners and their families aspired, symbolised by these simple but effective images.

We talk to one of the men carrying the old banner. He was a miner at Easington Colliery who travelled to work from Thornley. He is glowing with the pride and excitement of being accorded the honour of bearing the standard into Durham for the last time.

The Thornley group reaches the County Hotel, where at around 9am the guests of honour, including former Labour minister and fervent socialist Tony Benn, a regular at the Big Meeting, are already lining the balcony. Over a period of several hours, each lodge party, together with its band, banner and followers pause at the hotel and play for the speakers. Sometimes, as with the Thornley group, there are several banners under the 'umbrella' of one band.

Tony Benn
and other guests of
honour on the balcony
of the County Hotel,
2006

Photo by Tony Griffiths

The music performed is wide-ranging and includes arrangements of popular songs such as *Hey Jude* and *Don't Stop Me Now* as well as jazzy and Latin American-style pieces. Other melodies are more traditional, including such favourites as *The Blaydon Races* and the *William Tell Overture*. As the morning wears on and the sun comes out to grace the proceedings, the crowds thicken, a vast number clustering eagerly in the area around the County Hotel to watch the parade and identify the various guests on the balcony.

After each band finishes its performance, they and their banner and followers march away amid cheering and clapping down Old Elvet to the racecourse. Then the next group moves forward to take up position in front of the balcony, the bright colours and messages of their banner as much the centre of attention as the band and guests of honour.

Among the lodge parties is one from **Easington Colliery**. Thoughts of the 1951 disaster must surely surface in the minds of numerous onlookers. Fittingly, the band plays the beautiful and moving *Gresford*, the miners' hymn.

At the funeral of many of the Easington disaster victims, a Yugoslav diplomat laid a wreath at the gravesides in Easington Colliery cemetery. Attached to the wreath was a pennant version of his country's flag. Ever since then the miners of Easington Colliery have draped their banner with a Yugoslav pennant in acknowledgement of that tribute. This year is no exception. As well as the pennant, the front face of the banner shows the Easington Community Garden.

At a little before 2pm the Thornley contingent marches from the racecourse. The Area Band leads them down Old Elvet, across the bridge and then up towards the cathedral via Saddler Street and Owengate. Following behind are the other new banners to be dedicated and blessed: the banner of **Durham Aged Mineworkers' Homes Association**, and of **Handen Hold, Crookhall** and **Eppleton** collieries. The last three have their own groups of musicians, the Uppermill Brass Band, the Yorkshire Co-op Band and the Backwood Band.

The **Aged Miners' Homes** banner depicts bungalows built by the association and bears mottoes reading, "Labour and Love" and "Help One Another" as well as the message: "At The Heart of the Mining Community".

Photo by Richard Smith

The **Handen Hold Colliery** lodge banner (see colour section) carries a painting of the pithead and on the other side a portrait of Aneurin Bevan, the South Wales miner who as a Labour minister founded the National Health Service. The motto beneath the portrait reads, "Loyalty and Endurance".

The **Eppleton** standard depicts Hetton Hall and an early George Stephenson steam locomotive. The other side features the pithead winding wheel of Eppleton Colliery's Jane Shaft. In 1951, the same year as the Easington disaster, Eppleton suffered its own tragedy when nine miners were killed in an explosion.

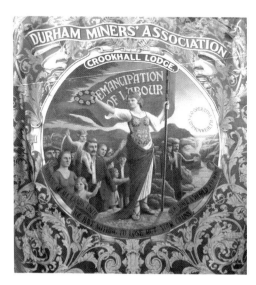

The new Crookhall Lodge banner
Photo by Richard Smith

The **Crookhall** banner depicts a female figure carrying a flag inscribed with the words "Emancipation of Labour". She is leading a group of men, women and children towards a better life, inspired by the ideals of socialism, which is a traditional image. The other side features a design based upon the spokes of a pithead wheel with images showing the Aged Miners' Homes at Delves Lane, the Victory Pithead with the colliery band in front, a miner, the entrance to the Woodside Winnings drift mine, Crook Hall mansion and the old Delves Lane County Junior School.

We position ourselves behind the old Thornley banner as the group awaits the signal to enter the cathedral by its main door, preceded by the NUM Area Band. Lining up behind is the new standard with its picture of the cathedral and church and the colourful little banner of Thornley Primary School.

After a short time, we move slowly into the cathedral – lowering the banners and negotiating them through the modern inner doorway is a tricky procedure. After entering, we look around us to find hundreds of people packing the seats of the nave. The eyes of this huge congregation are firmly fixed on the band, the little group from Thornley and its standards. The band play a soft air which sounds out majestically throughout the great building It is a heart-stirring moment as we walk up the aisle to the head of the nave where senior clerics, including the Bishop of Durham and the Dean, are waiting to welcome us.

One by one the other bands and banners enter by the north doorway, with its replica Sanctuary Knocker, and proceed up the aisle beneath the lofty ceiling to the accompaniment of their own, equally stirring music. It is clear that the entry of the banners is a solemn but beautiful moment, which all present are thrilled to witness. One of the cathedral stewards draws our attention to the 1893 Haswell banner high on the wall of the South Transept, (see colour section). The pioneering union leaders depicted on this standard would surely have been delighted that the annual service begun in 1897 is still being held more than 100 years later.

The voice of **Billy Middleton** now breaks the expectant silence. He speaks as the representative of the Thornley community, formally asking the Bishop to dedicate the new banner as a symbol of the fellowship and service of the local people. In turn, the representatives of the Durham Aged Mineworkers' Homes Association, and the Handen Hold, Crookhall and Eppleton communities ask the Bishop the same question. The Bishop replies that he is glad to, then dedicates and blesses the five standards "that they may bear witness to the selfless devotion" of the people of Thornley, the Aged Miners' Homes Association, Handen Hold, Crookhall and Eppleton and inspire everyone to lives of discipleship and service.

Thornley Banner
Photo by Richard Smith

The service ends with the singing of *O God Our Help in Ages Past*. The procession of bands and banners then leaves the cathedral, to the traditional medley of jaunty airs. Members of the congregation clap in time to the music, fully enjoying the spirit of the occasion. Thornley's standards are borne through the great doorway and then past Palace Green bathed in sunshine and down the hill to the city's main streets, where already the departure of the banners and bands from the racecourse is well under way. Brass music once more fills the narrow streets as the crowds enjoy the march-out.

The public houses are doing a roaring trade and groups of happy people stand or sit outside with their beers, enjoying this wonderful finale to a day of sheer excitement. More than 40,000 well-wishers have attended the event and over eighty banners and forty bands have paraded through the city. It may not equal the attendances of fifty years ago, but it is nevertheless remarkable in a coalfield where all the deep mines have closed. We walk back to the Gala field and witness the last contingent passing down Old Elvet, the musicians still playing with the same gusto they displayed in the morning. The field is almost deserted, but next year it will stir again to this unsurpassed gathering of the coalfield's people.

THE GREATEST HONOUR

Gala organiser George Robson stresses the camaraderie inherent in coal mining when he explains the event's appeal and its survival despite the closure of every pit in County Durham.

What makes the Durham Miners' Gala a success? Many times I've had that question put to me. Why have the mining communities of the so-called Great Northern Coalfield not allowed this celebration of their history and heritage to wither and die like so many of the other areas in the country where coal was mined for generation after generation – with annual galas celebrated accordingly?

The answer is simple, though in my opinion multi-faceted. For 125 years miners and their families have marched into Durham on Big Meeting day and celebrated their culture with a camaraderie unique to coal mining. This camaraderie especially felt by those who worked underground in dark, dirty and often dangerous conditions led to friendships that were forged for life. This comradeship with their marras (workmates) and fellow miners locally, nationally and even internationally I'm sure became the envy of most working people.

Although the industry has been lost – the last pit in Durham having been closed in 1993 – perhaps a determination not to lose this camaraderie still prevails and the Gala provides a celebration of this. So many miners I know meet old marras in the same pub or club in Durham for the crack, just once a year on the second Saturday in July. To them this day, as many have said, is better than Christmas Day – a poignant statement indeed.

Certainly a great passion is evident from the community groups and lodges of the DMA, a passion not to forget their history and heritage. After all, most of the villages in the old County of Durham proliferated because of the finding and winning of coals under their feet. What better way to celebrate the very existence of their community by marching into Durham behind their banner and a brass band, and in effect saying: "Governments and economics may well get rid of our industry, but look we are still here, active as a community, alive and kicking, look at our banner, listen to our band.

George points to other facets of the event's success: the ancient city of Durham with its historic charm and character; the natural amphitheatre of the old racecourse with funfair, entertainment and speeches; the backdrop of the magnificent cathedral and the Miners' Festival Service. But the camaraderie and community feeling provide the occasion with its spirit.

Tony Benn and the Gala – "*I would not miss it for the world*"

Photo by Tony Griffiths

Those who do not come from mining families may also be moved by this spirit. They include ardent socialist and former Labour MP and Minister **Tony Benn**, who famously gave up his hereditary peerage. An honorary member of the NUM, he has spoken on the platform at the racecourse many times.

Mr Benn served as Minister of Technology, Secretary of State for Industry and Secretary of State for Energy. He represented Chesterfield – a mining constituency – during the Great Strike of 1984-85 and spoke up for the miners on many occasions in Britain and abroad, raising money for them.

I first heard about the Gala from Hugh Dalton who was then the MP for Bishop Auckland and he said: 'The greatest honour anyone in the labour movement can receive is to be invited to speak at the Durham Gala.' Therefore I was extremely excited when at the age of 37 I was invited to do just that by Sam Watson, then the general secretary of the Durham NUM.

He told me that I had been chosen by ballot among the miners and I think one of the reasons I was asked was that I was in the middle of fighting my battle to get out of the House of Lords, which had attracted a certain amount of public attention and a lot of support in the movement.

Unfortunately the invitation was addressed to me as 'Lord Stansgate' and I wrote to Sam that as I was engaged in the battle to get rid of the title I couldn't agree to speak under that name. He replied to say that as the name Lord Stansgate had been printed on the ballot paper he had no alternative but to insist that I did.

Given that I realised what a huge honour it was, it was with enormous regret that I wrote back to say that if he insisted I would be unable to accept, fearing that this supreme opportunity would pass, and to my delight he half conceded by writing to me as 'Anthony Wedgwood Benn (Lord Stansgate)' and on that basis I travelled to Durham.

All the guests were put up at the County Hotel, as they still are, and I went to the pre-Gala dinner which was attended by Hugh Gaitskell, George Brown, and many other leaders of the movement. I was advised to get up early in the morning to go on to the balcony as the bands and banners started passing the hotel very early. And it was – and still is – a very moving occasion.

I seem to recall that at the time there were over 120 pits still open and anyone who has stood there as I have done over the past 45 years and seen the colliery bands march in, stop, play to those on the balcony and then march off towards the racecourse, will have been struck by the fact that all human life is there, with the miners' families and children, and old and disabled miners in wheelchairs, and the streets packed to greet the beautiful banners which they carry.

Spirit of the Gala

Former colliery bricklayer, George Rowe, holds the Lambton Lodge banner after rising from his wheelchair at the 2008 Big Meeting, helped by his friend, Billy Middleton. George died in October 2008.

Photo by Richard Smith

These banners of course are decorated with the greatest figures in the movement, including Tommy Hepburn, Keir Hardie, George Lansbury and some of the great miners' leaders going back to the General Strike and beyond.

In those days there were two platforms on the racecourse, to accommodate the size of the crowd and the number of speakers and, in the blazing sunshine, it was a festival of solidarity for which there is no parallel – the greatest event the labour movement has.

The speeches were all serious and passionate and the platforms contained all the local Members of Parliament, including the party leader who always spoke every year, until Neil Kinnock withdrew following the demonstration against him in 1989 when the bands marched off during his speech as a mark of their anger that he was not supporting the miners in their historic struggle against Thatcher's pit closures.

After the meeting, the guests were always invited back to the hotel for a meal, but of course the service in Durham Cathedral takes place then and to hear a colliery band in the cathedral is one of the most moving experiences of my life. It provides an opportunity for preachers to connect the history and aspirations of the movement with the Christian teaching of peace and brotherhood.

I was deeply touched that the NUM should still invite me to come, even though I am no longer a speaker and it is a date I pencil into my diary every January because I would not miss it for the world.

Today of course the faces on the banners include people I knew personally, like Michael Foot, Dennis Skinner and Hugh Dalton. And when an invitation came to me to have my likeness put on the Blackhall Lodge banner, along with Keir Hardie, A.J. Cook and Nye Bevan, it was by far the greatest honour that I have ever received in my life and I said I would rather have that honour than a peerage – and didn't have to prove it.

Despite the massive pit closures, and the agony the miners experienced in 1984-85, the Gala flourishes and now attracts banners from other coalfields and other unions and invites Labour leaders from across the world.

For me it is a family gathering, in the greatest family in the world – the family of mineworkers, of which I am very proud now to be an honorary member with the membership number 001.

Dr Stafford Linsley remembers the Gala

Industrial archaeologist **Dr Stafford Linsley** comes from a County Durham mining family stretching back at least three generations. He grew up in the mining village of Boldon Colliery, where his father was a deputy at the pit. His great grandfather, Thomas Linsley senior, was an Independent Methodist preacher. In 1885, at the age of 31, Thomas was killed by a fall of stone while working at Monkwearmouth Colliery. Dr Linsley has memories of the Big Meeting going back many years:

I am not at all certain when I first attended a Durham Miners' Gala; moreover, I am very aware that memory can easily be infected by imagination and wishful thinking. However, that being said, I probably went to my first Gala during the late 1950s, when in my mid-teens. Although I was born into a coal mining family in Boldon Colliery there seems to have been no tradition of attendance at the Big Meeting amongst my immediate family members, but my 'Uncle' Joe Roberts, later to be Mayor of South Tyneside, was the Boldon Lodge secretary, and I probably went along with him.

Certainly, on one occasion, Uncle Joe asked me to help carry the Boldon banner, and although I felt privileged to do so, I soon learned that it was hard work in even the slightest breeze. I learned other things too. Many shop windows along the main streets of the city were boarded on the outside, not to prevent smash and grab thieves, but to protect the windows from the crush of the crowds; the easiest way to get to the racecourse was by following a band – the pavements were simply too crowded to get through that way; always take a rucksack for bits and pieces, rather than a carrier bag.

Dr Linsley remembers seeing DMA leader Sam Watson at the Gala on several occasions and he once got a sighting of Jack Lawson. Jack, like Sam, had been a miner at Boldon Colliery. He became MP for Chester-le-Street and served in the 1924, 1929 and 1945 Labour governments. When he retired from the Commons, the former pitman became vice-president of the National Parks Commission. Later, he went to the House of Lords as Baron Lawson of Beamish. In 1949, Jack became the first miner to be Lord Lieutenant of County Durham.

My father assured me Jack Lawson would be at the Gala, not as an 'honoured guest', but amongst the crowds following the banners, amongst 'his own'." This was confirmed when Dr Linsley caught sight of him *"walking behind a band and banner down Old Elvet with his bait tin in his hand".*

My memories of the Gala from the 1960s onwards largely merge indistinguishably. Amongst these were sixty or seventy brass bands perhaps, streaming into Old Elvet from three separate directions, their exhilarating cacophony of overlapping marching tunes assaulting the ears; the accompanying banners and supporters, together with the massed spectators crowding the narrow streets being the equivalent of the Fulwell End at Roker Park in the Sixties. But there were also reminders of the dangers in coal mining, for every year, before the rapid decline of the coal industry, one or more banners would be draped with black crepe.

Until the late 1980s you could be fairly sure that the leading members of the Labour Party and trades unions would speak from the platforms on the racecourse, but, characteristically Tony Blair and his New Labour project changed all that. Blair steadfastly avoided the Gala, even though he was part educated in Durham City and represented a former mining constituency.

But over the years I heard Aneurin Bevan, Bessie Braddock, Hugh Gaitskell, Richard Crossman, Jim Callaghan, Harold Wilson, George Brown, Barbara Castle, Michael Foot and others.

I did not always agree with what I heard, but I recall enthusiastically listening to a young Neil Kinnock, to Dennis Skinner at his sarcastic and incisive best, to an uncompromising Rodney Bickerstaffe and his 'Hypocrites' refrain, and to the brilliantly forensic journalist John Pilger. It was particularly moving, in 1995, to see John Hume, then leader of the SDLP, and one of my heroes, on the speakers' platform The Gala is infused with the political history of the United Kingdom of the past 140 years or so, and I for one remain constantly aware of this on Gala day.

Dr Linsley also has memories of the Miners' Festival Service:

A rather special occasion in the cathedral for me was in 1980 or 1981 when the Boldon Colliery band played a hymn tune, called 'Boldon', written by my father, James. He had spent 45 years working down the pit, and 60 years as organist at the local Independent Methodist chapel, but he was not at Durham to hear 'Boldon' played in the cathedral.

Dr Linsley and his wife have introduced the experience of the Big Meeting to friends who had never before witnessed it. "A special such occasion being when we took with us some Congolese women asylum-seekers who were gleefully astonished at the Morpeth Pipe Band and its 'men in dresses'."

Even though Durham's pits have now long been closed, pride in the Gala remains strong, and growing and welcome concern to celebrate mining heritage is now evidenced in stalls selling mining memorabilia, or advertising heritage groups such as the Durham Mining Museum, the Durham Miner Project etc. These, and presentations by a host of organisations ranging from the 'Durham Palestinian Solidarity Group' to 'Kick Racism out of Football' are sandwiched between the usual stalls offering candy-

floss, ice cream, toffee apples, fish and chips, tombola, haunted houses, etc.

Music on the racecourse now extends beyond the familiar brass bands to include folk, rock and jazz bands, some from overseas, such as, in recent years, a brass band from India and a male-voice choir from South Africa. All these interest groups and artists find their welcome place in a much more diverse Miners' Gala than in earlier years, and provide clear confirmation that the Gala remains an organically developing annual celebration.

What I have gradually come to realise is that the Big Meeting was, and remains, probably the most graphic illustration of the complexities of mining life above and below ground that it is possible to witness. The inspirational banners speak to us of history, hopes, fears, aspirations, and some industrial and social successes. The black crêpes remind us of the dangers of the work. The brass bands, the street dancing, and the crowds of people from former pit villages remain a tangible (and audible) demonstration of the talent, culture and exuberance always evident within mining communities.

The political speeches reflect the political interests of some, while the cathedral service reflects another kind of communal devotion. The stalls and marquees reveal the wide range of political affiliations held by some, and the charitable endeavours of others. The fairground is mainly provided for young people and children, important and valued elements of mining communities. The pubs, open all day, satisfy the thirsts of some, while the chapels, also open all day, provide tea, sandwiches and cakes as appropriate and adequate nourishment for others. The whole reveals a unity within apparently disparate elements of the North East's coal mining communities, a solidarity that transcends religion and politics. The Gala remains, for me, a glorious multi-layered pageant of the culture and complexity of Durham coal mining life, and it continues to provide an antidote to the folly of unfocused generalities on the nature of the working classes.

Monkwearmouth Lodge banner with its poignant
"Last Good Morning" theme on the racecourse in 1985
Photo Stafford Linsley

A TUNEFUL PICNIC

The Northumberland Miners' Picnic has a longer history than the Gala: the first Picnic to be officially listed by the miners' union was held on 11th June 1866, at Polly's Folly, also known as Polly's Field, between Shankhouse, now part of north eastern Cramlington, and Bog Houses.

"It would seem that Polly's Field was close to the site of the former Albion Inn at Shankhouse. The inn was known as *The Folly,*" says **Dr Eric Wade**, Senior Research Fellow in Mining History with the Open University. Dr Wade was an apprentice mining surveyor in the collieries of the Broomhill district, near Amble, for three years during the 1950s; his father was a pit deputy and active trade unionist. He admits, however, that the exact location of the Picnic seems to have been lost in the mists of time and the field may now be covered by roads, housing or other development.

It was on Christmas Day 1862, four years before the first Picnic, that a large number of Northumberland pitmen met at Horton, near Blyth, and decided to form a trade union. Accordingly, in January the following year a group of miners' delegates met at the Victoria Hotel, Newcastle. At this stage it seems they were all from Northumberland, but not long afterwards a number of Durham collieries joined the new union. However, this joint organisation did not last long, since in 1864 the Northumberland miners seceded from their Durham counterparts and formed their own union, known as the Northumberland Miners' Mutual Confident Association, a title generally shortened to the Northumberland Miners' Association.

The first officially listed Picnic was therefore held only two years after the foundation of the Northumberland Miners' Association, although it seems that a few informal picnics took place in the years immediately preceding the election of Thomas Burt as union leader in 1865. The event, like the Durham Gala, became an annual fixture, and in the same way it became an occasion for demonstrating the comradeship and unity of the miners as well as an expression of the friendly spirit and closeness of their communities.

Fewer banners and people attended the Picnic, but this reflected only the smaller size of the Northumberland coalfield. The event, which almost always took place in June or July, was nevertheless of great importance to the county's miners and families. The gathering was held only once at Polly's Folly. After this, many Picnics took place on the Northumberland coast at Blyth Links and inland at Morpeth, where Carlisle Park was the scene for the meeting. Several others were held at Newcastle and Tynemouth. Blyth and Newbiggin-by-the-Sea also feature in the list.

In 1919 there were two Picnics – one at Hexham and the other at Morpeth. This double arrangement was repeated the following year, with Hexham and Morpeth again being chosen. Afterwards, there was a permanent return to one Picnic a year, with Morpeth being very frequently selected. Then, from 1952 onwards, Bedlington became the favourite venue. Indeed, the event was held in Bedlington year after year until 1991 with the exception of the Great Strike of 1984-5 when it was cancelled and during the years 1979-81 when Ashington was chosen. From 1992, Ashington became the venue.

Northumberland Miners' Picnic procession, marching through Bedlington with the NUM Cambois Branch banner and brass band
Reproduced with permission of William Ward and Northumberland Collections Service

Accompanied by union branch banners, the colliery bands marched to the Picnic field. In Bedlington, this was at the town's Attlee Park, but before the march, the bands competed for honours in a keenly fought annual contest. To win the championship trophy, the *Burt Challenge Cup*, was a prestigious achievement; the musicians put in many hours of practice before the big day. Ellington, North Seaton, Cowpen & Crofton, Backworth and Ashington were among the bands which enjoyed great success in gaining this coveted honour.

The brass musicians and contingents of miners with banners, their families, and friends came from all corners of the Northumberland coalfield, converging on the chosen venue in the same way as they did in County Durham. At Bedlington, crowds would gather in the main street to see the bands perform in the competition before they marched off to Attlee Park.

Undated photograph of Clement Attlee and others
at the Northumberland Miners' Picnic
Reproduced with permission of William Ward and Northumberland Collections Service

A Picnic beauty queen was chosen and she would ride on a carnival-style float in the parade. On reaching Attlee Park, families sat down to an open-air meal on the grass. The funfair, situated in a separate field, proved a major attraction. Prominent Labour politicians and trade union leaders delivered speeches to the crowd from the park's bandstand.

Dr Wade, who was a geological, economics and education adviser to the NUM, recalls a visit to the Picnic by **Prime Minister Harold Wilson** in the 1960s. "After his speech I was invited to join him at Netherton Working Men's Club for a pint. The union always held lunch and tea at the club on Picnic day."

Miner **John Douds**, of Seaton Sluice, helped to carry the Bedlington 'A' Pit banner at the Picnic of 1970, the year before this colliery closed. He describes the experience as "exhilarating", with the crowds cheering on the marchers and people dancing in front of the banner. John's group set off from outside the Bedlington 'A' pithead baths at Bedlington Station and marched over a mile to the centre of Bedlington. He reflects that "the Picnic was the highlight of the year".

Bill Bell, a council member of the North of England Institute of Mining and Mechanical Engineers based at Neville Hall, Newcastle, was a miner at Ashington Colliery in the late 1960s. He has memories of the Picnic as a boy and it is clear that the feelings he had then for this important event are undiminished by time.

As I grow older I become more proficient in the art of time travel and have experienced it many times in both sight and sound. The sight of a colliery banner that once paraded through my home town of Ashington on its way to the Northumberland Miners'

Picnic held in the nearby town of Bedlington. The sound that heralded the bands – the thump, thump, thump of the bass drum. It was the signal for the music to swell forth and so did the hearts of those that heard it. Those followers of their respective collieries, families and individuals eager to march behind the banner and show their allegiance – they were as fiercely proud of their colliery as any ship's crew are of a vessel or soldiers of a regiment.

Today the sight of a banner or the sound of a bass drum instantly transports me through time to forty years ago when as a young man I saw the procession pass by on its way to that carnival day of band contests, where mysterious judges listened to the musicians through open upper windows lest any charge of bias be levelled against them.

Of course, I did not realise I was witnessing the beginning of the end, the end of a period of great social history, of a way of life and community cohesion and of an industry without parallel in its effect upon the nation. What other endeavour could match its strength? For without coal no wheel could turn and the railway, the mill and shipyard would lie idle for want of power.

John Brannan, of Lynemouth, was a miner for 34 years, working at Pegswood, Lynemouth and Ellington collieries. In 1961, he joined the Ellington Colliery Band as a tenor horn player. His wife, Winnie, was already a member; her instrument was the trombone. "My wife joined the band in 1953. There were very few women players in those days," he says. "We met when I was at Pegswood Colliery. She worked in the mine offices." He recalls Picnic day:

It was enjoyable for the musicians, but very tiring. We would set off about 7.30am playing and marching from one end of Lynemouth village to the other. Then we boarded a double-decker bus which took us to Ashington where we again played, parading through the town. Here we were joined by the other bands of the Ashington Mineworkers' Federation.

Then we got back on the bus and headed for the Picnic at Bedlington. Before the competition, which took place in front of the council chambers in the main street, we assembled outside one of the pubs for some last-minute practice. After the contest the banners and bands formed up in line and marched down to Attlee Park for the speeches. Following these, the results of the competition were announced and presentations made.

Northumberland Miners' Picnic 1956
Prize winning colliery band with NUM North Seaton Branch banner
Reproduced with permission of William Ward and Northumberland Collections Service

As well as the Burt Challenge Cup, there were many other trophies to be won. These included a cup for the winner of a contest for bands from outside the Northumberland area. The Durham coalfield provided most of the entries in this section.

Awards were also presented for individual instrument playing. When John first joined the band those winning these individual trophies received medals too. He tells of one year when there was a result which surprised him: "The adjudicator announced that members of the Ellington band had won nine out of the 10 individual awards available. The band, however, had failed to win the Burt Challenge Cup."

John comes from a mining family; his brothers and his father were also pitmen. Music runs in the family too. His older brother and an uncle played in the Pegswood Colliery Band. John was one of the last miners to play in the Ellington group, which is now sponsored by Northumbrian Water and known appropriately as the Northumbrian Water Ellington Colliery Band. His wife Winnie is still the band's treasurer.

Other talented groups which can trace their origins to the mines include Wansbeck's Ashington Colliery Band, which still has some musicians who were pitmen, and the Backworth Colliery Band, which no longer has former miners in its ranks, but continues to uphold the proud tradition of the coalfield's music.

George Brown, of Bedlington Station, is a former Ellington miner and bandsmen who played at the Picnic many times; his instrument was the euphonium. "It was a day of melodies," he says, recalling some of the pieces played at the event. They included *Gresford, Raby, Knight Templar, Death or Glory, The Middy, Imperial Echoes, Mephistopheles* and *The Cossack*.

Miner's daughter **Sue Coultard** came from the village of Linton. It was a small community, a little isolated from others in the surrounding area. Linton Colliery was part of the Ashington group of mines. All the men in her family worked in the pit, even if some only did so for a short period. Although her father was a union member and contributed greatly to the social life of the village such as helping with sports days, he was not very much involved with union social events such as the Picnic. Sue recollects that she rarely went to the Picnic with her parents. Instead, she attended with other members of her family and friends.

Linton did not have its own colliery band which meant there was no coach, so they had to make their own way to the Picnic on public transport; they caught a bus to Ashington and then another to Bedlington. The women of the village would pack up a picnic of homemade plate pies and cakes. A lot of effort went into providing the food for the family picnic.

Sue's lasting impressions of the event are from her early teenage years. "It was a big day out. An adventure without my parents and with my friends, lots of families, men and young people. They were all enjoying a big trip out."

She remembers seeing the bandsmen in their uniforms outside the pubs and clubs. They were gathering, each group often outside the same pub or club each year, for last-minute rehearsals before the contests. After the competitions large numbers of people watched the bands and banners march down the hill to Attlee Park.

Sue continues: "I didn't listen to the speeches much, though I do remember sitting on a grassy bank and watching a speaker, and while he addressed the crowd he was throwing his arms about a lot. We used to go to the amusement field even though this meant walking back up the hill for about 20 minutes!" When it was time to go home there was always a long queue for the buses. "Many people had enjoyed a drink during the day and a few did get drunk, but they were always happy and jovial. There was no malevolence. I always felt safe."

Dennis Murphy Snr, Joe Gormley, Sam Scott and Michael Foot
at the Northumberland Miners' Picnic in Ashington c.1980
Reproduced with permission of William Ward and Northumberland Collections Service

Unlike the Gala, the Picnic has not survived the closure of the mines in its original form. The traditional event was last held at Ashington in 2000, when the band competition took place in the main street, Station Road, followed by a parade to what was then the *Woodhorn Colliery Museum*, now redeveloped to form the *Woodhorn Northumberland Museum and Archives*. The last winner of the Burt Challenge Cup was the Fishburn Band – the competition had been thrown open to bands from outside the Northumberland coalfield.

However, the old-style event has been replaced by an annual 'Picnic Weekend'. There is no band contest or parade of banners to a field. Rather, the new Picnic takes the form of a memorial lecture meeting organised by the NUM and a memorial service to all miners who lost their lives in the Northumberland pits. The first few services were held at Woodhorn, but in recent years they have taken place at Holy Sepulchre Church, Ashington. The service includes the laying of wreaths. In addition, a family fun day has twice been held at Woodhorn Museum as part of the weekend.

Among the surviving Northumberland miners' banners is one from the **Rising Sun Colliery** which shows a view of the No. 3 coal-drawing shaft. It bears the motto "Safety Always". The reverse side displays the image of a rising sun with the names of several closed collieries from which men had transferred to the Rising Sun. **Ray Grew**, who was a miner at this pit in the 1960s, was among the men who marched behind the banner at the Picnic. He recalls that buses picked the miners up from outside their Welfare building in Station Road, Wallsend, to take them to Bedlington. The Rising Sun employed around 1,700 men underground, so the contingent was a sizeable one. "I don't think I ever missed a Picnic during my time at the colliery. It was a smashing day. We looked forward to it every year".

Ray, who still lives close to the site of the mine in the northern area of Wallsend, remembers the banner being paraded at the Picnic very shortly before the colliery closed in 1969. It was draped in black crêpe in remembrance of the last man to be killed at the pit, an accident that happened in February of the same year. Experienced face worker **George Fatkin** was felled by a fall of stone, having worked at the mine since 1947.

George Shepherd, who also lives near the site of the Rising Sun, was a 'marra' of Ray's. He recalls that each year a draw was held on the morning of the Picnic to determine which miners would have the honour of carrying the banner.

"The banner carriers received a full shift payment from the union," says George. "The draw was held at the Welfare before we set off for Bedlington. I was lucky enough to be one of the winners." The buses took the men to the ex-servicemen's club in Bedlington where they enjoyed drinks before the parade.

Like their Durham counterparts, some of the Northumberland banners display paintings of leaders or politicians admired by the miners. A portrait of Labour pioneer Keir Hardie takes pride of place on the **West Sleekburn** banner, with the inscription "His vision was our inspiration". The reverse side carries an illustration of the pithead baths. The **Seaton Burn and Brenkley** banner features the words "Retain the Old Unity", the word "unity" framed by four miners' picks.

A Bedlington Doctor Pit banner shows a miner and his family looking up at an angel in the sky wearing a sash bearing the words "Labour Party". A rising sun indicates the dawn of a better standard of life and improved working conditions. This side also carries portraits of **Robert Smillie**, the Scottish pitmen's leader who became president of the MFGB, and **Thomas Burt**, the most famous of the early Northumberland miners' union leaders.

Thomas Burt

Burt was born near North Shields in 1837 and began work at Haswell

Colliery at the age of ten. Other pits where he worked included Seaton Delaval, New Hartley, Choppington and Cramlington. He was elected leader only a year after the foundation of the Northumberland Miners' Mutual Confident Association. In 1874, he became one of the first two miners elected to Parliament – as a Radical Labour candidate with Liberal support. He was thus a 'Lib-Lab' MP and never joined the Labour Party in the early 1900s. His constituency was Morpeth.

Thomas Burt, known to most people as Tommy, was well liked. A skilled negotiator and speaker, by all accounts he was a witty and good-natured man. One journalist, writing in the 1890s, declared that the pitmen's leader was "plain spoken only when he sees that a straight word of counsel may help his brother, but he is never censorious, and there is always a kindly brotherliness about him".

Of his chairmanship of the Trades Union Congress meeting in 1891 an observer wrote, "The adroitness, the tact, the nimble-wittedness, and the good nature and self-possession which characterised him are beyond praise".

In 1892 Liberal prime minister William Gladstone appointed Burt as Parliamentary Secretary to the Board of Trade and he served in this post for three years. He had started his working life as a trapper boy opening and closing ventilation doors in the utter darkness of a mine and had risen to become a member of the government.

The former Northumberland miners' union headquarters, Burt Hall in Newcastle, now part of Northumbria University, was named in his honour. Appropriately, the building, which was opened in 1895, is topped by the statue of a miner carrying a pick.

Statue of a miner carrying a pick on the roof of Burt Hall
former offices of the Northumberland Miners Union
now part of Northumbria University
Photo by AIG

A Pegswood branch banner shows a crowd of people around a pithead on the day Britain's mines were nationalised. It carries the words, "Vesting Day, Jan 1ˢᵗ 1947." One of the buildings shown has a notice which reads, "This colliery is managed by the NCB on behalf of the people". The other side features a central portrait of **William Straker**, who was general secretary of the Northumberland miners' union from 1913 to 1935. He is surrounded by portraits of Labour pioneer **Keir Hardie**, president of the Miners' Federation of Great Britain (MFGB) **Robert Smillie**, Labour stalwart **Emanuel Shinwell** and **A.J. Cook**, who led the miners during the General Strike and Great Lockout of 1926. The message reads, "They

Blazed the Trail". This indicates the role these leaders played in advocating common ownership of the mines. As Minister of Fuel and Power in the Labour government elected in 1945, Emanuel Shinwell – known to all as "Manny" – did not just advocate common ownership; he was responsible for introducing the nationalisation measure and for its implementation.

William Straker

Taken from photo by Derrik Scott

William Straker's contribution to the Northumberland miners' union as their general secretary was exemplary. He was a moderate who believed in negotiation as the key to solving disputes rather than strikes. A Christian socialist and Primitive Methodist, he was also a pacifist who spoke out against the First World War.

Dr Wade, who is the honorary secretary of the North of England Institute of Mining and Mechanical Engineers, writes of him, "His role in changing working conditions in the mines and the promotion of education for all is a legacy which is still being felt".

Straker started pit work as a teenager at Widdrington Colliery with his father and a brother. Later, he moved to Pegswood Colliery where he was employed as a hewer at the coalface. As a young man he became active in the Northumberland Miners' Mutual Confident Association and was elected a member of the county executive of the union in 1882 at the age of 27. He was appointed general secretary in 1913 and was the first Northumberland representative on the national executive of the MFGB.

Perhaps Straker's finest hour came when on behalf of the MFGB he gave persuasive evidence in favour of nationalisation to the Sankey Commission. The commission brought out a report in 1919 which came down in favour of nationalisation, although the government did not accept the idea.

The hard-working leader also found time to actively promote better education, housing and health facilities in the North East. For example, he served on the governing bodies of the Royal Victoria Infirmary, Newcastle, and the city's Armstrong College, a forerunner of Newcastle University. He was also a trustee of the Professorial Chair of Mining at the college. The former pitman undoubtedly had great energy, for in addition he played an important role in the Northumberland Aged Mineworkers' Homes Association and served as a co-opted member of Northumberland Education Committee. Straker was made a CBE in 1930, an honour recorded on the Pegswood banner. In 2008, a commemorative plaque to him was unveiled on the facade of Burt Hall.

Dr Wade adds, "William Straker was passionate about achieving better working conditions for the miners and having been one himself for many years, working alongside his brothers, and having two close relatives killed in mining accidents he had empathy with their suffering".

Pegswood's is not the only banner to take up the theme of public ownership. An Ashington Mineworkers' Federation NUM standard of 1949 shows a miner and his family looking towards a pithead with the word "Nationalisation" above it. The other side features views of the five collieries in the Ashington Mineworkers' Federation. Ashington is in the middle, the others being Ellington, Woodhorn, Linton and Lynemouth. Later banners of the federation repeated these themes.

An **Ellington NUM** branch banner of 1950 carries scenes by Oliver Kilbourn, a member of the renowned Ashington Group of pitmen painters. One side shows a sombre view of colliery housing seen through the frame of a pit ventilation door, which is about to close. The motto reads, "Close the door on past dreariness". The other side depicts new homes in a bright tree-lined street, seen through an open door, with the words, "Open it to future brightness".

Hartford Hall, former convalescent home for injured miners, as it is today
Photo by AIG

Many of the surviving Northumberland banners are now kept at Woodhorn Museum and Archives Centre on the outskirts of Ashington. The centre occupies the site of the former Woodhorn Colliery, which closed in 1981, and is well worth a visit to see the banners and many other coal mining artifacts.

Photographs from the late 1950s and early 1960s taken by **Derrik Scott** show yet more banners, their whereabouts today unknown. A **Hartford Colliery** branch standard carries a painting of Hartford Hall, between Cramlington and Bedlington, the convalescent home for injured Northumberland miners (see colour section). It indicates that the lives and wellbeing of all the area's pitmen are "cherished" through the work of the home. A banner from **Netherton Colliery** shows a globe of the world flanked by two miners and surmounted by a family, with (below) miners working at a coal face. The message declares: "We unite to assist each other."

Holy Sepulchre Church in Ashington is packed with people for the Northumberland Miners' Memorial Service at the Picnic Weekend of June 2009. The sunlight floods into the spacious church, which stands only a few streets away from the site of **Ashington Colliery,** which closed in 1988. A wide cross section of the former mining community is represented in the congregation, including the young and the elderly, men, women and children.

The Ellington Colliery branch banner is positioned on one side of the altar and on the other is the standard of the Ashington Federation of Collieries. Between them, suspended from the ceiling, is a wooden cross.

Wansbeck's Ashington Colliery Band begins the service with an impressive rendering of *When the Stars Begin to Fall.* It is now that many in the congregation recognise one of the clerics processing towards the cross: it is an old friend of the miners, the Rt Rev Dr David Jenkins, the former

Bishop of Durham who twenty five years earlier spoke out against the government's determination to defeat the miners and called for a humane settlement during the Great Strike, stressing the need for compromise. The Rev Elizabeth Bland introduces the service, recalling the church's strong and abiding connection with the pitmen and their families.

The service also includes the singing of the hymn *Colours of the Day* by children from Welbeck First School, Ashington, and a reading by Stephen Thompson of verses from Psalm 139.

An address is then given by Wansbeck MP Denis Murphy, who tells of the appalling conditions which early pitmen faced, of the New Hartley pit disaster and the progress made by the miners' unions in improving conditions following those dark days of the 19th Century. He speaks of great pitmen's leaders Tommy Hepburn and Thomas Burt.

After more prayers, led by the Rev Lorna Beadle, members of Ashington & District Male Voice Choir perform *Take Me Home* and *Colliers Requiem* from *Fell 'Em Doon* by Mike Kirkup and Derek Hobbs. These songs are poignant reminders of the pit closures and of a vanished way of life.

Dr Jenkins then addresses the congregation. Towards the end of a short but at times witty sermon, in which he speaks of the 1984-85 strike, he reminds the congregation of the Parable of the Good Samaritan. Warm clapping follows his address. Here is a man who has clearly won the hearts of the community.

The laying of wreaths in front of the altar follows, introduced by former Ellington Colliery miner **Neil Taylor**. These floral tributes commemorate those who lost their lives in the pits of the Northumberland coalfield.

Ian Lavery, a former Ellington miner and president of the National Union of Mineworkers, lays the first wreath, on behalf of the union. Among others laying floral tributes are Viscount Ridley, who is a former Lord Lieutenant of Northumberland, DMA general secretary Dave Hopper on behalf of the NUM North East Area and Dennis Murphy MP. Wreaths are also laid on behalf of various branches and sections of the NUM and the Northumberland Mechanics. Other unions are represented too – the Healthcare branch of Northern Unison, the Fire Brigades Union, and the Northern TUC, as well as the Labour Party.

The Bevin Boys lay their tribute – some are present in the congregation. Other wreaths include those from Browell, Smith & Co, solicitors, the Northumberland Aged Mineworkers' Homes Association, Hirst Welfare and Northumberland County Council.

After the ceremony is completed, around 25 floral tributes adorn the space below the cross. All those present observe two minutes' silence in remembrance of the departed. Fittingly, Wansbeck's Ashington Colliery Band then plays *Gresford*, the miners' hymn, during which the congregation stands.

Afterwards Mr Lavery makes presentations to Welbeck First School children. He tells the congregation that mining is not all "doom and gloom" and stresses that miners have good times as well as bad. He adds that coal mining is not finished – he believes it will stage a comeback. The service ends with a fine rendition by the band of *The Waters of Tyne*.

At the Northumberland Miners' Picnic family day event at Woodhorn Museum there are fairground rides, other amusements, children's face-painting, a hooky and proggy mat making demonstration, and performances from Wansbeck's Ashington Colliery Band. There are also performances from The Cyber Pitmen – musicians dressed as robots on stilts and wearing miners' helmets – by Beeswing, a group providing traditional music and songs, and by the Monkseaton Morris Men. In addition, a craft fair takes place in one of the old colliery buildings. Thus the Picnic is continuing into the 21st Century as a celebration of Northumberland's mining heritage and one cannot help feeling that the miners of yesteryear would warmly approve.

A new Northumberland Area NUM banner, a first for the whole Area, was dedicated at Woodhorn in 2007. It was the result of a joint project between the NUM, the Northumberland Aged Mineworkers' Homes Association and Northumberland County Council with the help of the Heritage Lottery Fund. Young people were involved in the scheme. This impressive new banner was inspired by one dating from the early 1920s carried by miners of the Ashington Federation of Collieries. On one side it features a female figure carrying a torch as she leads a miner wearing shorts and other workmen towards "The New Vision" of a better life for workers and their families. She points to a group of children dancing around a maypole with the words "Gain the Co-operative Commonwealth" above them. The maypole ribbons bear the words "Beauty, Fellowship, Health, Art and Science." The motto declares: "Workers of the World Unite".

The other side carries what is perhaps the strongest imagery of any throughout the North East coalfield: a group of miners carry a coffin in a funeral procession from a colliery. Some of the men are injured. The pit is on fire. However, emerging from the blazing pit shaft is the giant figure of a man who is pointing a spear labelled, "State Control" towards a fire-breathing dragon symbolising profit and private ownership. The man is clearly about to slay the dragon of capitalism.

The message on the banner reads, "The workers' industrial union and his own political Labour Party will destroy this monster", which is a call for nationalisation of the mines, indicating that health and safety should be put before profit. The motto repeats the wording of the original banner of the 1920s, a time when the miners were pressing for common ownership of the industry.

Front cover of Ashington Collieries Magazine, 1923
From private collection

IN MEMORIAM

The issue of health and safety has always been a central one in the coal industry. Explosions, flooding, roof falls, transport accidents and industrial diseases engendered by dust led to the deaths of thousands of men and boys who worked in the North East mines. Scattered throughout the Great Northern Coalfield are memorials to the large numbers who lost their lives in the numerous pit disasters, including such major tragedies as New Hartley, West Stanley, Seaham, Wallsend, Haswell, Felling and Easington.

Methane gas – known to the miners as 'firedamp' – was the most common cause of such large-scale loss of life. When exposed to naked lights or sparks, the presence of this gas can lead to devastating explosions. In addition, carbon monoxide gas – known as 'afterdamp' – often forms in the aftermath of such conflagrations and can prove as deadly as the initial blast. However, improved safety measures gradually reduced the overall death tolls from accidents. Much better ventilation with powerful electric fans and the introduction of hydraulic steel pit props were among the factors which helped to bring the figures down.

Tributes to those who died in large-scale disasters are not the only memorials. They have also been erected to individual collieries and their miners, including all who lost their lives at the pit. These memorials take various forms, but among the favourite symbols are the pithead winding wheel, the safety lamp and the coal tub. However, whatever form a tribute takes it becomes a focal point which people can visit to remember the miners.

Ellington was the last deep mine in the North East. It closed in January 2005, so ending around 800 years of coal mining in the region, apart from a few opencast sites. It is an extreme irony that coal is now imported into the ports of Tyne and Blyth. This really is a case of 'coals to Newcastle'.

In 2008, a winding wheel from Ellington was erected at the eastern entrance to **Westerhope** Village in Newcastle. This impressive survivor from the region's last deep mine stands as a memorial to nearby **North Walbottle Colliery** and its pitmen. The wheel was officially presented to the Westerhope community by NUM president Ian Lavery. A rare sight was the North Walbottle banner, which was brought from Woodhorn especially for the occasion. Its mottoes read, "Let Brotherly Love Continue" and "Unity is Strength".

The year 2008 also saw the re-dedication of a memorial to the thirteen miners killed in an explosion at **Woodhorn Colliery**, Northumberland, in 1916. It takes the form of a white obelisk surmounted by the fine statue of a pitman holding a safety lamp and pick. For many years this impressive sculpture graced Ashington Village's Hirst Park, before being moved in 1991 to Woodhorn. Eleven of the thirteen men who died in the Woodhorn accident were married, with thirty four children between them. One had returned from the Great War. However, in the worst tragedies to hit the coalfield the numbers killed reached treble figures.

The churchyard at **Earsdon**, between Shiremoor and West Monkseaton, features the memorial to the 204 men and boys who died in the **New Hartley Colliery** disaster of 1862, the largest death toll of all the North East pit accidents. Several of the boys lost in the accident were aged ten. Unusually, the tragedy was not caused by an explosion or flooding, but by part of a cast iron pumping engine beam breaking and falling down the pit's single shaft, carrying with it a mass of debris, and thus blocking the only means of escape for the miners working below. The face of the memorial is inscribed with the names of all those who died. One older miner perished with three of his sons and a grandson.

Four miles away from Earsdon, in the village of **New Hartley** itself, the capped pit shaft and another plaque can be found in a small memorial garden. The New Hartley disaster led Parliament to pass an Act which stipulated that all mines should have at least two shafts so that an alternative means of escape was possible. It also led to the setting up of the Northumberland and Durham Miners' Permanent Relief Fund, which provided payments to the widows and families of men killed in pit accidents, on the condition the men concerned had contributed to the fund from their wages.

The main memorial to the second worst North East pit disaster can be found at the eastern end of the High Street in **Stanley**, County Durham, close to Slaidburn Road. It commemorates the 168 men and boys who died as the result of an explosion and its aftermath at **West Stanley Colliery** in 1909: fifty nine of the 168 victims were aged under twenty. The West Stanley memorial features two impressive 'half' pit winding wheels and the names of the victims, together with the names of the seams they were working in on the day of the tragedy. In front, a mosaic 'carpet' depicts a safety lamp, a miner's shovel and a pick. The memorial was unveiled in 1995 by former Newcastle United manager Kevin Keegan, a grandson of one of the rescuers. A plaque makes clear the tribute is "also dedicated to all miners and their communities".

West Stanley Colliery Disaster Memorial
Photo by Tom Yellowley

In 2009, the centenary year of the disaster, a remembrance service for those who died was held at St Andrew's Church, Stanley. The church was packed with people, including descendants of victims. A second service took place at the memorial on the exact anniversary of the tragedy, February 16, when the bells of St Andrew's were rung a symbolic 168 times.

THE HUNDREDTH
MINERS' FESTIVAL SERVICE

We attended the 100th Miners' Festival Service in Durham Cathedral on July 11, 2009. Appropriately in the centenary year of the disaster, the West Stanley banner was among the standards carried into the great building on this most special of occasions. Also present was the banner of Easington Colliery. These two standards represented the communities hit by the worst North East pit disasters of the 20th Century.

For the 100th time the colourful banners of the miners were borne up the great aisle and the sound of brass music from colliery bands echoed through the cathedral. The wonderful melodies were provided by the musicians of the Durham Miners' Association Band, Easington Colliery Band, Westoe Brass Band, Layburn Brass Band, Huddersfield Brass Youth Ensemble Band and Dobcross Silver Band.

We entered with the contingent accompanying the Easington Colliery banner. As always, every seat in the cathedral was occupied with people eager to take part in this unique event. As we marched towards the head of the nave, the Easington Colliery Band played *Gresford*.

The three new banners dedicated and blessed by Bishop Tom Wright were those of Boldon, Westoe and South Hetton lodges, all of which were made by Chippenham Designs.

The **Boldon** banner is a typical example of a contemporary miners' standard, displaying both old and new images. One side depicts a traditional theme celebrating nationalisation of the mines in 1947 – a miner representing "Tyrannicide" holds hands with a female figure representing "Trust". The pitman – complete with cap lamp, knee pads and pneumatic pick – has just triumphed over the "dragon" of private ownership. A competition was held between six schools in the Boldon area to choose a design for the reverse side. The judge, professional banner-maker John Midgley of Chippenham Designs, selected a motif from the children of East Boldon Primary School featuring a series of images which the children associate with coal mining. These two themes unite the heritage of the pits and the younger generation. The mining images are grouped around a central silhouette of the Boldon pithead and include a pick, shovel, pitmen, a pony and tub, safety lamp and a coal fire in a home. "Progress through learning" reads the motto.

The **Westoe** banner displays on one side a view of the Westoe pithead at South Shields seen from the inside of an old school window. Next to this is a view of the new Westoe Crown Primary School, seen through the window of a modern classroom. The two images are based on ideas supplied by children from the school. North East artist and former miner Bob Olley helped greatly with the project, developing the design from the children's concepts. The school, together with a housing development, was built on the site of the mine. The motto reads, "Their future is built on our past". Another inscription declares, "Education for all". The other side of the standard shows the tower of Westoe Colliery's Crown Shaft and the pithead wheels of the old St Hilda Colliery at South Shields. The motto declares, "Remember our heritage with pride". As with the Boldon standard, Westoe's themes bring together the mining past and the younger generation.

The new Westoe Lodge banner on the racecourse, 2009
Photo by Jean Smith

The **South Hetton** banner has a picture based on a mural at the village community centre. It depicts the colliery's pithead and a group of miners. The message states, "Lest we forget those who went before us". The reverse side displays the socialist "Emancipation of Labour" theme with its hope of a better life for the pitmen and their families.

During the service, the West Stanley and Easington Colliery banners were moved to the crossing of the nave and transepts, becoming a focal point as the choir sang an anthem, followed by a voluntary played by the Durham Miners' Association Band. The final hymn of the service, *Jerusalem*, was sung with particular enthusiasm. As always, the banners and bands marched out to lively tunes, in contrast to the earlier solemnity, with the congregation clapping in time to the music.

The 2009 Gala, the 125th, proved to be a resounding success amid brilliant sunshine. The attendance was estimated to be the highest in thirty years. Seventy or more miners' banners, a host of standards from other trade unions and about sixty bands took part in the parade, including musicians from France and Mexico; the procession to the racecourse lasted around five hours. One of the most venerable banners on show was from Leasingthorne lodge; it was first unfurled in 1950.

People danced in the streets, sang, laughed, cheered, clapped and sometimes felt tears welling into their eyes. They met old and new friends. Bands gave impromptu concerts to the crowds lining the way, on the march into Durham and on the march out. In celebratory mood, the people responded with warm applause. Spontaneous enjoyment ruled the day.

As we left the old city amid the music, the colour and the friendly atmosphere, we felt our lives to have been enhanced by this extraordinary day. We felt certain that the miners will never be forgotten by the people of the North East. It is hard to see how it could be otherwise. They remember with affection and respect their comrades, fathers and forefathers whose arduous labour underground in conditions of danger fuelled Britain's industries and gave warmth and light to the homes of millions. The banners and bands of the Gala and Picnic have ensured that the spirit of those miners shines out with an enduring brightness.

AUTHORS' ACKNOWLEDGEMENTS

The authors gratefully acknowledge and wish to thank the following people for their kind help in the preparation of this book: Dave Hopper, Dave Guy, George Robson, Jack Fletcher, Tony Benn, the Vice-Dean of Durham Cathedral the Rev Canon Dr David Kennedy, the former Bishop of Durham the Right Rev Dr David Jenkins, Dr Tom Yellowley, Richard Smith, Tony Griffiths, Bob Bach, John Attle, Norman Emery, Bob Herrick, Mick Tilley, Lin Gatiss, Terry Meadows, Pat Simmons, Dr Stafford Linsley, Jim Wilson, Derrik Scott, Bryan Scott, Bob Melvin, Derek Gillum, John Taylor, Mike Syer, Alan Cummings, John Robson, Billy Elliott, Billy Middleton, Bob Ord, Ian Lavery, Lynn Camsell, Dr Eric Wade, John Douds, Bill Bell, Ray Grew, George Shepherd, Michael Fatkin, John Brannan, Sue Coulthard, Deborah Welch, Tom Peacock, Jeff Gobin, John Watson, Arnold Ellis and George Brown.

Ergo Press would like to thank Durham County Council and the Fire Brigades Union for their generous support in the publication of this book.

BIBLIOGRAPHY

The Big Meeting: A People's View of the Durham Miners' Gala
Edited by Keith Armstrong (1994)
Northumberland Miners' History 1919-1939, J. Davison (1973)
*Follow the Banner. An Illustrated Catalogue of the Northumberland Miners'
Banners,* Hazel Edwards (1997)
Banners of the Durham Coalfield, Norman Emery (1998)
The Coalminers of Durham, Norman Emery (1998)
Durham Cathedral: Light of the North, John Field (2006)
*The Miners of Northumberland and Durham: A History of their Social and
Political Progress,* Richard Fynes (1873)
The Durham Miners 1919-1960, W.R. Garside (1971)
Banners & Brass: Images of Durham Miners' Gala, Dave Jamieson (2007)
The Banner Book, W.A. Moyes (1974)
The Durham Miners' Gala 1935-1960, Michael Richardson (2001)
The Great Northern Miners, Ken and Jean Smith (2008)
A History of the Durham Miners' Association 1870-1904, John Wilson
(1908)